"I'm always thinking about how to make this world a better place, more joyful, a place where there's real fulfillment and excitement about life. When we have people like Nicole mentoring women, I am more optimistic about the future. She is a model of enthusiasm; she has the great ability of taking any 'ashes' from her past and turning them into beauty. She can write, speak, act, and bring the ordinary experiences of life into focus, giving hope with humor and wit. Bottom line, her advice will take you to new heights of encouragement."

—Dr. Gary Smalley
Best-selling author and speaker

"I really love coffee! So the minute you say 'fresh brewed" I'm ready to fill my cup. In *Fresh-Brewed Life,* with gentle determination Nicole Johnson helps us to really examine our hearts, our minds, our relationships—yes, even our souls. This is an invitation to a life filled with meaning and purpose. So, open these pages with expectancy, and pour yourself a rich, deep, satisfying cup of fresh-brewed life."

—Terry Meeuwsen
Cohost, *The 700 Club*

"There are days when a smooth French vanilla latte hits the spot: one sip and I'm ready to take on the world. And, then there are those mornings when it takes old Juan Valdez himself—and his pack mule—to drag me from my house. At last, Nicole Johnson gives us a *fresh* cup of brew—with all the benefits of a strong cup of coffee—only without the caffeine!"

—Chonda Pierce
Comedian and Recording Artist
Myrrh Records

I have shared many cups of coffee, longings, celebrations, and life's lessons with this powerful writer and speaker. You will be challenged by her honesty, her humor, and her questions. Find a silent place, get comfy, and get ready to savor the aroma of truth that is released in every page.

—Esther Burroughs
Author and Speaker

Fresh-Brewed LIFE

A Stirring Invitation to Wake Up Your Soul

Nicole Johnson

THOMAS NELSON PUBLISHERS®

Nashville

Published in Nashville, Tennessee, by Thomas Nelson, Inc.

Scripture quotations are from the HOLY BIBLE: NEW INTERNATIONAL VERSION®. Copyright © 1973, 1978, 1984 by International Bible Society. Used by permission of Zondervan Publishing House. All rights reserved.

An exhaustive search was done to determine whether previously published material included in this book required permission to reprint. If there has been an error, a correction will be made on subsequent editions.

Excerpts from *Simple Abundance* by Sarah Ban Breathnach. Copyright © 1997 by Sarah Ban Breathnach. By permission of Warner Books, Inc.

Excerpt from *The Face of Love* by Ellen Zetzel Lambert. Copyright © 1995 by Ellen Zetzel Lambert. Reprinted by permission of Beacon Press, Boston.

Excerpts from *Why Beauty Matters*, Karen Lee-Thorp and Cynthia Hicks, © 1997. Used by permission of NavPress/Piñon Press. All rights reserved.

"That's What the Lonely Is For" by Dave Wilcox. © 1993 Irving Music, Inc. (BMI) & Midnight Ocean Bonfire Music (BMI). All rights reserved. Used by permission. Warner Bros. Publications U.S. Inc., Miami, FL 33014.

Recipes are excerpted from *The Coffee Book* by Christie Katona and Tom Katona, published by Bristol Publishing © 1992. Used by permission of Bristol Publishing Enterprises, Inc. All rights reserved.

"A Story to Live By" by Ann Wells in the *Los Angeles Times* © 1997. Reprinted by permission.

ISBN 0-7394-1717-7

Printed in the United States of America

Contents

Special Thanks

Fresh-Brewed Life would be an unopened, vacuum-sealed bag of beans on a shelf somewhere if it were not for the amazing urging and contributions of the following people.

To Robert Wolgemuth, literary agent and friend, for the encouragement to use my voice.

To Mike Hyatt and Thomas Nelson with gratitude for believing in that voice.

To my celebrating friends: Audrey, Angela, and Denise and other special people in my life who took time to pray, read, and reflect this book back to me. John, Betty, Ken, and Esther, thank you for drinking cups of Fresh-Brewed Life this year.

To our Advisory Board for continued wisdom and counsel, but most of all, for the bellows of encouragement to keep the fire of passion glowing.

To my trusted associate and friend, Mary Bowman, who handles more details of my life than I do. Thank you for sharing this journey with me.

To my mother, for loving deeply enough to encourage me to write our story and for living freely enough to allow me to share it.

Introduction
TAKING YOUR FIRST SIP

Awake, my soul! (Psalm 57:8)
I have come that they may have life, and have it
to the full. (John 10:10)

"Would you like coffee this morning?" I love those words. When I am on the road traveling or staying in someone's home or just out for breakfast, those six words bring life to my day. When I am home, usually whoever gets up first, me or my husband, Paul, puts on the coffee. Hearing the sound of coffee brewing, I dance when I smell the aroma filling my kitchen.

The dark liquid in the cup transcends simply being water poured over ground-up beans. Coffee is far more than a beverage. It is an invitation to life, disguised as a cup of warm liquid. It's a trumpet wake-up call or a gentle rousing hand on your shoulder. Coffee is lingering scent, better than any potpourri. Coffee is an experience, an offer, a rite of passage, a good excuse to get together. When someone invites you to get coffee, it isn't because they're thirsty. It might be because they're cold, but more likely it is because they want to spend time with you. Coffee makes a promise.

> ## Ten signs you know you need a wake-up call to a fresh-brewed life:
>
> 1. You yelled at your minister last Sunday, or ever.
> 2. You fell asleep at your own party.
> 3. You lobby for chocolate to be one of the four food groups.
> 4. Your husband doesn't want sex, and you're happy about that.
> 5. You called your best friend and started chatting, and she said, "Who is this?"
> 6. The people you work with are asking when your next vacation is.
> 7. Your kids look forward to going to school.
> 8. Your idea of a good time is a coma.
> 9. You can't remember your last vacation.
> 10. You agreed to serve God, but only in an advisory capacity.

Here's the promise of a fresh-brewed life: the Almighty wants to spend time with you, stirring your soul and waking you up. He is inviting you to embrace a fresh-brewed existence. "Fresh-brewed" makes a guarantee: this life will not be stale. This is not the freeze-dried stuff your grandmother drank. This is not Sanka. This is the real McCoy—authentic, energizing, stimulating.

I need truth in strong doses like a great cup of coffee in the morning. I need to hear from God and be changed, every day. It's not caffeine that does that. I drink mostly decaf, but coffee still wakes me up in the morning. It's the experience. It's the Lord God Himself bringing the opportunity for refreshing and stillness. You can't drink coffee quickly. You hold it, you sit with it, and you savor it.

Coffee also calls us out of hiding. When someone puts on a pot of coffee, people come from everywhere. It draws us out of our usual hangouts into the center of activity. I need to be drawn out of my own little world, and so do you. I see women all the time who seem joyless and lonely—I can see it in their expressionless eyes. They stare straight ahead or look down, walking forward but not going anywhere, They are terrified that life is going to find them.

I heard the story of a mother was telling her little girl what her own childhood was like. "We used to skate outside on a pond. I had a swing made from a tire; it hung from a tree in our front yard. We rode our pony. We picked wild raspberries in the woods." The little girl was wide-eyed, taking this in. At last she said, "I sure wish I'd gotten to know you sooner!"

> "May you live all the days of your life."
> —Jonathan Swift

Where have we gone as we've grown up? Let's get reacquainted with ourselves. We've been dulled by life and all our responsibilities. We are reacting to our circumstances instead of purposefully engaging them. You may not even know you've been asleep, until the stirring begins.

SARK wrote in *Succulent Wild Woman*,

It is tempting to sleepwalk through life. To tell half-truths, listen half-way, be half-asleep, drive with half attention . . . Wake up! We need you as an alive and awake woman, listening and contributing. Wake up your creative genius and let it out into the world. Wake up to your power and use it wisely. Wake up to your pain and investigate it. Wake up the dull old parts that are hiding from the light. Wake up to love and let it flood through you.

Now that you've awakened . . . immediately take a nap!

This is a fresh-brewed life. Waking up, and then napping. Napping is not sleeping. It's giving yourself a gift. Being kind to your soul. Taking off your impossible-to-please hat and putting on a feather boa. Joining your life that is already in progress. Agreeing to be an active participator instead of a silent spectator. Saying yes to making a difference in this world.

> "Life is either a daring adventure or nothing."
> —Helen Keller

Fresh-Brewed Life is a journey of awakenings:

- To our God, by responding to His passionate love for us

- To ourselves, by embracing our identity in Christ and letting it spill over into our every corner

- To others, by relating in new ways that bring joy and release the aroma of life!

People who don't even like coffee usually love the smell and the experience. I have friends who don't drink coffee, but they never pass up the opportunity to go to get some. It's the place, the people, and the passion. They will have hot chocolate or a smoothie or some beverage, just to embrace the invitation to get together. Even if you don't drink coffee, this book still holds the same promise: wake up to a better life.

Coffee is a universal welcome. It is available to all of us, rich or poor. It doesn't matter what country you live in, what language you speak—you can get a cup of coffee without much trouble. I have had coffee in almost all fifty states and in eleven different countries. I have friends who have sipped cups in England and others who have been served coffee sitting in a grass hut in the desert of Oman. The message is always the same: friendship and warmth. You are welcome here.

We only live once, and if we do it well, once is enough. This book holds nine cups of fresh-brewed life to wake us up. Remember, you have to sit with coffee a while, so take one cup at a time, over the next nine days, nine weeks, or nine months. Get a journal, go on the "fresh-brewed adventures" in each chapter, use the percolations, and enjoy the recipes. And I humbly promise you, if you give this book nine months, God will birth something incredible in your life. You will discover a richer, fuller, more flavorful and meaningful existence.

> I have measured out my life in coffee spoons."
>
> —T.S. Eliot

One
SURRENDER
TO GOD

*Y*ou reach for the brass door handle and pull. The seal of the door is broken, and the vacuum-packed freshness envelops your senses. You step inside and the warmth wraps around your soul like a wool scarf. Your whole body is enveloped by the aroma. Hearing the familiar hissing of steam works on your stress level like a pressure valve. You've entered a coffee shop, and you're helpless. You give yourself to it. Surrender.

You're staying in the home of a good friend. You have no responsibilities this morning, so you just wake up on your own. You blink and focus your eyes. Your clothes are lying across the chair. The sunlight is streaming in through the window, and it plays on the corner of the bedspread. Then, from downstairs, the invitation finds you. Your nose has discovered the promise of a wonderful day, the smell of fresh-brewed coffee. It draws you out from under the covers, and you pull on clothes as you make your way toward the promise. Surrender.

She's sitting in the chair she always sits in. She's been

2

awake for hours. From the time you were little, you can remember her being up before everyone else. She has her Bible open and her coffee cup in her hands. Peaceful and calm. The warmth of her spirit is matched only by the warmth of your love for her. Her heavenly Father and a cup of coffee. She knows Him, and He knows her. Surrender.

The fresh-brewed life is a spiritual journey from beginning to end. It is a call to wake up that begins in a relationship with the One in whom we began. He alone is the One who can tell us what we most want to know. He alone is the Rock strong enough to anchor our lives in the midst of storms. He, and only He, is enough to rouse our sleepy souls.

I cannot rouse my sleepy soul. I tried getting up at four-thirty in the morning to have a quiet time with the Lord. Trust me, it was quiet. I have fallen asleep on God on more occasions than I can count. I have tried to memorize chapters of Scripture and found that I've killed so many brain cells with Nutra-Sweet trying to be thin and holy that I'm no longer able. I thought that Jesus said, "Come unto Me, all you who are weary and heavy laden, and I will give you more to *do* than anyone else!" But Jesus didn't say that. He promised me rest. But I couldn't find it. My constant struggle to be "godly" left me tired, empty, lonely on the inside, and ready to give up.

I was either going to take pretending to a whole new level or quit pretending altogether, and I wasn't sure which. I deeply identified with the story of *The Emperor's New Clothes.* I felt like the king who was pretending that he saw the invisible clothes when there were no clothes. I was so afraid to let go of my pretense and be honest that I was tired and empty. In the story, everyone thought the emperor was naked, but they, too, held on to pretending. It took a little boy at the parade to wake them all up. The higher our level of pretending, the farther we have to fall. I did not want to be exposed. No one does.

Joan spent all of the first day of her vacation sunbathing on the roof of her hotel. She wore a bathing suit that first day, but on the second, she decided that no one could see her way up there, and she slipped out of it for an overall tan.

She'd hardly begun when she heard someone running up the stairs. She was lying on her stomach, so she just pulled a towel over her backside.

"Excuse me, Miss," said the flustered assistant manager of the hotel, out of breath from running up the stairs. "The Hilton doesn't mind your sunbathing on the roof, but we'd appreciate your wearing a bathing suit as you did yesterday."

"What difference does it make?" Joan asked calmly. "No one can see me up here, and besides, I'm covered with a towel."

"Not exactly," said the embarrassed gentleman. "You're lying on the dining room skylight."

Talk about exposed! It's terrifying until you realize one thing: when you're naked, you've got nothing to hide anymore. When you're empty, you have nothing else to be taken away. When you tell the truth, it sets you free. So, I made my decision to stop pretending.

I gave up. I surrendered. My whole-bean self. I let go. I stopped being in charge of my spiritual goodness, because I didn't have any spiritual goodness. I had worked for God and yet withheld my heart from Him. I'd sought to please Him, like a father who is hard to please, and missed that He was pleased with me. I tried to do so many things *for* God that I missed being *with* God. Where was the goodness in that? I was the keeper of the covenant. I was the one making the sacrifice. I thought what Jesus did for me paled in comparison to what I was doing for Him! God was so pleased to see me surrender, He probably laughed. I think He got tired just watching me. I

4

discovered that the Christian life is not about trying harder. It is not about keeping it all together. It is about trusting in the One who can keep it all together. Martin Luther said that we show whether or not we believe the gospel by what we do when we sin. If we just roll up our sleeves and try harder, we are not walking with Jesus. If we can do it all ourselves, what do we need Him for?

> "I'm discovering that a spiritual journey is a lot like a poem. You don't merely recite a poem or analyze it intellectually. You dance it, sing it, cry it, feel it on your skin and in your bones. You move with it and feel its caress. It falls on you like a teardrop or wraps around you like a smile. It lives in the heart and the body as well as the spirit and the head."
> —Sue Monk Kidd, *When the Heart Waits*

When I gave up, I began to wake up. I felt the gentle stirring in my soul to respond to God. He whispered to me, "Jesus came to give you life." *Life? What is life if it isn't running all the time?* Peace—real peace on the inside, from all of this climbing, striving, and worrying. Joy—unabashed delight in life, regardless of the circumstances. Love—foundational, unconditional, never-ending love. I didn't have to work for these things, I just had to surrender to them. I had to stop long enough to let them overtake me. Again and again.

This first cup of fresh-brewed life is the most important cup in the whole book. Surrendering to God is the key that unlocks the door to the life you want. A bigger spiritual "to do" list or a calendar full of church activities will not change our lives. When we give ourselves to God—mind, body, soul, and spirit—*He* changes us. We cannot change ourselves. We don't have enough spiritual stamina to change ourselves, let alone another person or the world. But when the walls come down and He has access to the deepest parts of who we are, His love courses through us in a cleansing, holy way. And we are dif-

ferent because of it. Stronger, richer. As different as instant coffee is from fresh-brewed. We become a full cup of steaming,
inviting life.

𝒫ercolations

Books
> *The Trivialization of God*, Donald McCullough
> *Dangerous Wonder*, Mike Yaconelli
> *Clinging: The Experience of Prayer*, Emilie Griffin
> *The Sacred Romance*, Brent Curtis and John Eldredge

Movies
> *Mrs. Doubtfire*
> *Leap of Faith*
> *Les Miserables*
> *The Mission*

Music
> *Wakened by the Wind*, Susan Ashton
> *Kansas*, Jennifer Knapp
> *Holy Land of the Broken Heart*, Michael Kelly Blanchard

Discovering in Christ the Whole-Bean Essence of Who We Are

> *"What is my only comfort in life and death?
> That I belong body and soul to my faithful sav-
> ior Jesus Christ."*
>
> —Heidelberg Catechism

After putting her children to bed, a mother changed into old
slacks and a droopy blouse, took off her makeup, and proceeded
to wash her hair. As she heard the children getting more and

6

more rambunctious, her patience grew thin. At last she threw a towel around her head and stormed into their room, putting them back to bed with stern warnings. As she left the room, she heard her three-year-old say with a trembling voice, "Who was that?"

I wonder the same thing about myself! Between dress-up evenings, afternoon runs to the grocery store in sweats, and stay-in-my-pajamas-and-work mornings, I stay in wardrobe confusion. From changing diapers to exchanging business cards to rearranging furniture, the tasks that we perform during the day are no help in determining who we are. We can *do* anything, but that doesn't mean we want it to define us. Bringing home the bacon, frying it up in the pan, changing a flat on the way home, starting to feel like I'm a man! But I'm a woooman. No wonder we are confused about who we are.

Emilie Griffin in *Clinging: The Experience of Prayer* tells us,

> He is the one who can tell us the reason for our existence, our place in the scheme of things, our real identity. It is an identity we can't discover for ourselves, that others can't discover in us—the mystery of who we really are. How we have chased around the world for answers to that riddle, looked in the eyes of others for some hint, some clue, hunted in the multiple worlds of pleasure and experience and self-fulfillment for some glimpse, some revelation, some wisdom, some authority to tell us our right name and our true destination.

Who am I? Have you ever lain awake at night asking that question? I take that back. Most women work too hard to miss sleep by lying awake at night, much less asking questions! So the questions probably come at other times. *Who am I?* Do you ever feel that you're faking your life? That you're living someone else's life, and you're not sure whose? You wonder how you got to this place of disguise. You want to give yourself to God, but what self are you going to give?

Your work life? What you do doesn't determine who you are. Your beauty? What you wear, or the hairstyle you sport, or how much makeup you have on isn't necessarily the "real you." Your relationships? All your roles as wife, mother, and friend are not the sum total of your identity. So what do we give and who are we?

The answer is (D), all of the above.

We are like onions. We can't merely peel away all the layers, because they are us, as long as they are true to the core. You don't get to the middle of an onion and find an apple core. The onion begins at the core, and each and every layer builds upon the "onion-ness" inside. An authentic life and self is one in which the layers on the outside are merely expressions of the core on the inside.

The core on the inside is what we surrender to God. I tried to work my way from the outside of the onion in. Doing spiritual things, dressing a certain way, trying to be a submissive wife—all of those things are external things that don't define the core; they reflect the core. Our identity is not determined by these things.

For example, our dogs drink out of the toilet. I'm "oversharing" here, but there is a point to this. They eat out of a dog bowl, and they eliminate waste outdoors. Now, if tomorrow I began to drink out of the toilet and eat out of a dog bowl and go to the bathroom outside, would you think that I was a dog? You might think I was confused, but you would not think I was a dog. You would notice instantly the discrepancy between the inside core (human) and the outside behavior (dog).

What you do doesn't determine who you are in the core of your being, but it does reflect what you believe to be at the core of your being. No one acts inconsistently with who they see themselves to be. Remember Hans Christian Andersen's story of *The*

Ugly Duckling? The duckling was bitten and made fun of for being so ugly. He was utterly miserable. He tried everything to be a better duck and to "fit in" with the animals in the barnyard. Then he saw his reflection. He wasn't a duck at all; he was a swan. A beautiful, graceful swan. Swans make terrible ducks, and even worse chickens, and if it were even possible, they wouldn't be very good cats. All of which the duckling tried to be. It wasn't until he discovered the core that the externals made sense. His inner identity changed his outer activity. It moved him from striving to resting. It changed him from trying to prove his worth to accepting his value. In short, he became a believer in the One who made him because he finally understood who he was.

In *Clinging*, Emilie Griffin cleared up this mystery:

There is only One who can tell us this: the Lord himself. And He wants to tell us, He has made us to know our reason for being and to be led by it. But it is a secret He will entrust to us only when we ask, and then in His own way and His own time. He will whisper it to us not in the mad rush and fever of our striving and our fierce determination to be someone, but rather when we are content to rest in Him, to put ourselves into His keeping, into His hands. Most delightfully of all, it is a secret He will tell us slowly and sweetly, when we are willing to spend time with Him: time with Him who is beyond all time.

> "A quiet spirit is one in which all of those mixed emotions are sorted out, understood, shared with trusted friends, and submitted to a spirit of contentment. The butterflies in our stomachs don't die; we just teach them to fly in formation."
> —Karen Lee-Thorp and Cynthia Hicks, *Why Beauty Matters*

Surrendering to God the whole-bean essence of who we are will allow Him to whisper that secret to us. Like seeing your reflection for the first time, God will reveal to you the truth about who you are. Several years ago, God used a little book called *Life of the Beloved* by Henri Nouwen to whisper to me: "'You are the Beloved,' and all I hope is that you can hear these words as spoken to you with all the tenderness and force that love can hold. My only desire is to make these words reverberate in every corner of your being—'You are the Beloved.'"

That, my sisters, is our deepest identity. We are loved passionately by God. And I don't know why. It is a mystery, and it must remain a mystery. To understand it is to dismiss it as we are prone to dismiss every other love in our lives. If we discovered that God loved us because we were smart, then we would try to do everything we could to be smarter so He would love us more. If we met someone smarter than we are, we would fall into despair. We couldn't believe God would love us if we weren't the smartest. So I don't think God will ever let us know the reason that He loves us as passionately as He does. I don't have a clue why God loves me. But I believe in the core of my being that He does. So I surrender to it. I stop fighting it. I cease trying to figure it out. I collapse on it.

Nothing can take His love from us. I can say that of no other love. God pursues us, courts us, and woos us to remind us. His love changes every day; it either intensifies, or my understanding of it grows, but I don't think it really matters which it is. He doesn't get tired of us, and He isn't frustrated by our moods or by our appearance. His love is all we have ever dreamed of. We are free to place the whole weight of our identity on Him. He will not lean, crumble, struggle, stagger, or

"To dare to live alone is the rarest courage; since there are many who had [sic] rather meet their bitterest enemy in the field, than their own hearts in their closet."
—Charles Caleb Colton

falter in any way. His love is the answer to the questions of the culture. His embrace, the way to freedom. And His kiss, the most passionate we will ever know.

This love is why we were made.

Recipe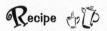

Coffee Mallow Parfait

24 regular-size marshmallows (about 3 cups)
1 cup double-strength coffee
1 cup whipping cream, whipped
1/2 cup chocolate cookie crumbs

In a medium saucepan combine the marshmallows and the coffee. Cook and stir over medium heat until marshmallows melt. Chill until partially set. Fold the whipped cream into the marshmallow mixture. Chill again until partially reset. In parfait glasses, start with the coffee/mallow mixture and layer the mixture with the cookie crumbs so that there are at least three layers of cookie crumbs. Top with the coffee/mallow mixture. Chill again till serving. Just before serving, add a dollop of whipped cream. Garnish, if desired, with a drizzle of Torani Mint or chocolate syrup, and top with a large chocolate shave or an Andes Mint candy.

Surrendering to Be Finely Ground

The darker the roast of the coffee, the more intense the flavor. It stands to reason that for a rich, strong life, we are going to have to go through the fire. This "roasting" can deepen our walk. The finer the grind of the beans, the more concentrated the coffee. First Peter 1:3 tells us that in His great mercy, God has given us new birth into a "living hope," through Jesus.

That's the identity we now have. We are children of God, and our hope is alive. "In this you greatly rejoice, though now for a little while you may have had to suffer grief in all kinds of trials." These trials have come, the Scripture says, "so that your faith—of greater worth than gold, which perishes even though refined by fire—may be proved genuine" (1 Peter 1:6–7). This genuine, refined by fire, holding-on-for-dear-life faith will result in praise and glory to Christ.

We are the beloved of God. We will go through trials, but we can submit to them so that our faith, the most precious thing we have, may be authentic. When people see our lives, they know we are honest people. Suffering makes us real, and that brings glory to God.

We were in Phoenix on business several years ago. I was checking messages before we headed out for the day. I was on my last message, and it was my sister: "Dad's had a heart attack. He's in the hospital . . ." Her voice was strong and steady; I knew she wouldn't want to frighten me. "He's in stable condition. They're still running tests." My heart was racing. I was thinking through how to cancel all that we had scheduled for the next several days to get to Alabama. "Everything is under control, and there's nothing you can do here, but please pray." My sister knew me. I appreciated her control and reassurances, but I had to get there. We canceled our business and got on a plane. Making so many fast decisions under the straining circumstances of Dad's condition was harder than I thought, and when I sat down in 23B, I started to cry. I was afraid. *What if something happens to him and you don't make it there in time? When was the last time you told him you loved him?* I sat in my seat weeping. The flight attendant brought me tissues and asked if she could help. I told her I was flying home to be with my dad, who had suffered a heart attack. She told me she had lost her dad two years previously, and we cried together. She did

Coffee represents 75 percent of all the caffeine consumed in the United States.

12

not make me feel better. The grinding got worse. But out of that experience I shared with her about Christ, and how I trusted Him, even if I didn't make it there. As I filed off the plane, I looked into more faces than I ever look into when I'm traveling. When we are in pain, we look for others who are in pain. I wondered how many people were on this plane whose loved ones were ill. I wondered why I never get on a plane looking for who might be hurting. Suffering has a way of opening our eyes.

In *Simple Abundance*, Sarah Ban Breathnach wrote, "It saddens me that many of us need to have pain as a wake-up call. Now I try my best not to stand on the sidelines of life with deadened, dulled, disinterested senses until another shock makes me suddenly aware of the magic, marvel and mystery of it all."

I made it to Nashville, and we drove five hours to the hospital. Nothing could have prepared me to see my strong, military father lying in a bed with a tube in his nose. I thought I had cried all my tears before I got there, but I was wrong. I thought I flew all that way to hold him, but I think I really needed him to hold me. And he did. His embrace alone told me that he would be OK.

Jesus prayed, "Not My will, but Thine be done." That's the most terrifying prayer in all of Scripture. God asks some very hard things of us. He asked Abraham to sacrifice Isaac; He let Lazarus die before Jesus raised him from the dead; He did not spare His own Son. God wastes nothing. Not our joys, not our sorrows—nothing. When we offer Him the whole-bean essence of ourselves and we submit to be finely ground, it will produce character in us. He knows the fragrance that comes

"Reading about prayer and praying are as different as reading a romance novel and kissing."
—Nicole Johnson

from surrender. He knows firsthand the return from the grain of wheat that falls to the ground and dies.

I think we only get to this kind of surrender through prayer. Just as Jesus did. We bring our lives to Him and wrestle them to the ground and let them go. Notice I didn't write, "bring your problems to Him and get over them." This is hard stuff. Don't be afraid to wrestle with God. It makes the surrender even more real and honest. Sometimes I pray with people who are afraid to be real. They are questioning God, or even angry, but their prayers sound very sweet: "God, I just know that You know what's best for me, so I just thank You for all that You've given me, and I just praise You for who You are." It's not my place to judge anyone's prayers, but I think God would be honored with a bit more honesty. He made our hearts, and He knows what's in them.

I love the story of the dinner party where the father asked his six-year-old daughter to bless the meal in front of their evening guests.

"But I don't know what to say," the little girl replied.

He coaxed her some more. "Just say what you've heard Mommy say."

"Dear Lord," she began, "why did I invite all these people to dinner?"

Exposed again. Can we trust that prayer is the safest place to tell the truth? Do we dare believe that God can hold all of who we are and more? Jesus said in John 8, "You will know the truth, and the truth will set you free" (v. 32). What better place to begin telling the truth than in our relationship with the God who loves us? This is true surrender, laying down your guns, false motives, and strategies at the feet of the One who has captured your heart. There is no shame at the feet of Jesus. No one can come and pull the curtain back and expose you because the curtain is already open. It's been torn from top to bottom.

14

Our prayers reveal our shortsightedness. When we pray and ask for specific things we want, we might be incredibly disappointed. But when we ask for the Lord's will or His presence, we always get our wish. Even more, we get what we are really longing for. We might pray for God to bring us a friend rather than praying for the strength to *be* a friend. We pray, "Lord, take this struggle away," rather than "Let this struggle produce in me endurance." Surrendering to be finely ground is bearable when we have the comfort that God is shaping us by our suffering, and He will not leave us or forsake us in the midst of it.

Are you awakened and opened by life's sorrows? Trusting that God will make something of all the pieces? Surrendering our agenda for our lives is the hardest thing we will do. I wish for you the willingness to look right at the hidden parts of yourself and allow honest exposure and confession to take place.

Directed Journaling

- What are some of the outside layers of your onion? Do they match the core of your being?
- Who are you when no one is looking?
- Have you been "kissed" by God? What did your life look like before the kiss? How is it different in the aftermath of that kiss?

Letting the Passionate Love of God Pour Through the Filters of Our Lives

Everyone else in the theater was laughing. They were slapping their knees and hooting. Paul and I were sniffling. We were watching Robin Williams in *Mrs. Doubtfire*. There were some fabulous, funny moments, but it was not a comedy. It was a passionate love story. We left the movie, but the movie didn't leave us. We had been deeply impacted by this movie, we thought, because of the pain and struggles in the divorced family. Pain that we both could relate to, having come from broken homes. We were touched by the passion of the father for his children. Two days later, the light came on: this movie was a retelling of the gospel.

Think about it. You have a father (Robin Williams) who was separated from his children. He wasn't allowed to see them except for one day a week, to which he cried, "One day is not enough for me!" He loved them so much that he dressed up as a nanny to get the job of housekeeper and cook. Every day, he became what he was not to demonstrate his love for them. When he was discovered, the same judge pronounced him crazy. The father protested that he did what he did out of love for his children. The judge said, "That's not love!" And Paul and I shouted, "Yes it is!"

In the language of Philippians 2:7 (my paraphrase), in reference to Christ, Paul wrote, "He disguised Himself, took on the form of a servant" so that He could be with His children. God became one of us to be near us and to demonstrate His unyielding passion for us. Jesus came not to be served, but to serve and to give His life as a ransom for many.

"Amazing love, how can it be, that Thou my God shouldst die for me?"

This kind of love calls us to respond with passion and intensity. "Love so amazing, so divine, demands my life, my soul, my all." God wants to dance with us. He does not want to give us a list of chores. The goal of dancing is *not* to learn the steps. The goal of dancing is to enjoy your partner. We learn the steps, but only so we don't have to look down at our feet. We are free to look into the eyes of the one we love.

I love Emilie Griffin's description of this passion in *Clinging:*

16

The Lord seizes us suddenly with a quick burst of affection. His power flows to us. He sweeps us up. Everything else stands still for a kiss that is passionate, tender, demanding. In anticipation of this kiss, whole lives are altered and overturned. In the aftermath of this kiss, destinies and ambitions and careers are discarded like old pairs of gloves. This is the sign of a love in which there is no disenchantment, no chance of boredom, no ultimate letdown. All is climax. This kiss is the pledge of a union that feeds and heals us, clothes and shelters us, that makes us Christ.

> "Usually, when the distractions of daily life deplete our energy, the first thing we eliminate is the thing we need the most: quiet, reflective time. Time to dream, time to think, time to contemplate what's working and what's not, so that we can make changes for the better."
> —Sarah Ban Breathnach, Simple Abundance

I spent too much time running from this kiss because I wasn't sure it was a kiss. I thought I was supposed to pursue God, not realizing that all the while, He was pursuing me. I saw God as the enemy of what I wanted rather than the fulfiller of my deepest needs. Many women over the ages have had such encounters with the living God.

I had no idea who he was the first time I laid eyes on him. His skin was dark, and he was beautiful. My heart skipped about four beats when he spoke to me. "Will you give me a drink?"

I swallowed hard. He knew that was forbidden. I thought maybe he was testing me to see what I would do. But his eyes gave him away. I knew immediately he wasn't talking about water. Something inside me stirred, and I had to look away.

When I turned back to him, his eyes were still fixed on

me. "If you knew who I am, you would ask me for a drink, and I would give you living water."

I couldn't breathe. He was offering to give me a drink. I knew he was a Hebrew, but love can make anything work. The way he was looking at me . . . "Sir," I stammered, "you have nothing to draw with, and the well is deep." My voice sounded shallow, and I felt like a child. "Where can I get this living water?" I asked him slowly, challenging.

He paused, holding my gaze as if it were my face in his hands. "Everyone who drinks this water will be thirsty again," he said as he glanced at the well. "But whoever drinks the water I give . . . will never thirst again."

Each word reached deeper inside me.

Never thirst again. Was he talking about what I thought he was? If he could only know how I thirsted. If he could only . . . he was staring at me, watching my every reaction. "Give me this water so that I won't get thirsty and have to keep coming here to draw water," I whispered.

"Go call your husband and come back."

I felt like he cared for me, and now he asked this thing of me. Was he mocking me? I stood my ground in shame. "I have no husband," I replied. Tears stung the sides of my eyes.

"You have told me the truth. I know that you have been with many men, and the one you are with now you don't love." His dark eyes were a sea of compassion as he looked at me with kindness. I was undone. I wanted to say something. I didn't want this conversation to end. I was suddenly afraid he would go away. He was right about my life; he was right about my thirst.

"You are a prophet." It was all I could think of to say. How else could he know so much about me?

God knows us and loves us passionately. He longs for us to allow Him to bring the living water and pour it over our lives. He did it two thousand years ago, and He still does it today.

18

Fresh-Brewed Adventures

- Spend time in the Psalms, especially when you are feeling finely ground. This amazing book of Scripture reminds us that we are not alone in our suffering. Rewrite some of the words to apply directly to your situation in order to find some of the comfort hidden there. For example, Psalm 61 says, "Hear my cry, O God; / listen to my prayer. / From the ends of the earth I call to you, / I call as my heart grows faint; / lead me to the rock that is higher than I. / For you have been my refuge, / a strong tower against the foe." You might write in your journal, "Do You hear me crying, O God? I believe You are listening to my prayer. In the middle of my kitchen I am calling You. I have lost heart. Lead me to a place where I can hope in something greater than myself. You have been that hope; let me climb to that high place again, where I can see and believe."

- Make a date with a hymnal. Borrow one from your church and take it with you to get a cup of coffee. Just sit and read some of the words to the great hymns of our faith. Or if you have a friend who plays the piano, get together to sing some.

- Set aside some time for stillness this week. Put it on the calendar. Work through the prayer section of this chapter, and bring your honest thoughts to God. Yield to Him, lay down all of your agendas, and just spend time with Him who is beyond all time. Give Him yourself for an hour.

Following the Process

God's love pouring over the grounds of our lives wakes us up to a more flavorful life than we ever could have imagined.

In Him, we understand the full essence of who we are. We find at last our true identity as deeply loved children. How we have longed for that all our lives, and we taste it in relationship with God. In Him, our sorrows are not wasted. As we submit to suffering as a path to real life, He pours His love over the grounds. The fragrant aroma, the warmth, and the satisfaction of a fresh-brewed life are the results of the process. It all takes place in Him.

But every step in the process is important.

One Sunday we were in a church performing, and we began singing with the congregation, "It Is Well with My Soul." This is one of my favorite hymns. It was born out of great loss, which makes it what it is: authentic and powerful. We sang loudly, "When peace like a river attendeth my way, / When sorrows like sea-billows roll; / Whatever my lot, Thou hast taught me to say, / 'It is well, it is well with my soul.'" I love this hymn. Then we sang the second verse, "Though Satan should buffet, tho' trials should come, / Let this blest assurance control, / That Christ has regarded my helpless estate, / And hath shed His own blood for my soul." Now we were getting somewhere—trials, surrender, it's all here. Powerful lyrics.

Then the minister of music dealt the death blow, "On the last . . ." *On the last? We can't sing the last verse without singing the third verse! You can't skip verses of "It Is Well with My Soul," especially if you know them!* Look at the words to the third verse: "My sin—O, the bliss of this glorious thought, / My sin—not in part but the whole, / Is nailed to the cross and I bear it no more, / Praise the Lord, praise the Lord, O my soul!" Yes, there is an exclamation point in the hymnal. Incredible verse, incredible hymn. The last verse begins with, "And, Lord, haste the day when the faith shall be sight." Well, I hated to tell the minister this, but you can't haste the day until you nail the sin! It will not be well with our soul if our sin, not in part but the whole, doesn't get nailed to the cross. If it doesn't get

Raw coffee beans, soaked in water and spices, are chewed like candy in many parts of Africa.

nailed, then we still bear it, and no one will be praising the Lord, much less hastening the day. Paul and I sang the third verse in rebellion! Quietly of course, while everyone else was hastening the day. The last verse really is wonderful, but it has to be in order. Here's how it goes: "And, Lord, haste the day when the faith shall be sight, / The clouds be rolled back as a scroll, / The trump shall resound and the Lord shall descend, / 'Even so'—it is well with my soul." Glorious, but you must keep the order straight.

So it is with the journey of fresh-brewed life. Starting with every piece of us—all that is lovely, hideous, fun, dry, sinful, beautiful—we surrender it to God. We allow the hard things we go through to make us better rather than bitter. God pours

> "And the day came when the risk [it took] to remain tight in the bud was more painful than the risk it took to blossom."
> —Anaïs Nin

His love over us, and we are changed. God's love can't pour over us until we are finely ground. It won't release in us any fragrance, or make any changes or any fresh-brewed anything. But when we are ground, we become more like Him, less like us. Coffee can't be made back into beans, but we find that what He has created surpasses what we started with.

Close your eyes. Think of something that makes you smile. A kindred-soul friendship, a delightful painting, a freshly bathed puppy. Smile deeply. Not with your mouth but with your soul. Breathe in, and smell the coffee. Feel the warmth and the promise of a fuller life by waking up.

What stage are you in right now? Are you crying uncle yet? Been exposed? Ready to give up? Ready to tell the truth and bring some honesty into your life? Are you longing to know the truth about who you are in Christ? Has your life turned out to be harder than you ever could have imagined? Can you still your heart to let God's love pour over you? This fresh-brewed journey is a circle. It doesn't end, it just begins again. We go back to the whole bean, we're ground by something else, and God meets us with His love to release a fragrant aroma.

With God guiding us, this book will be a holy safari into the dry terrain of heart and soul. With each cup we'll go deeper and deeper into our souls. When we get to the driest, deadest parts, we're going to run through the sprinkler and let sweet, refreshing water splash us and wake us up.

ENCOUNTER
YOUR JOURNAL

*T*uesday, *September 15, 1998*

> *I feel so uninspired to write today. Do I really have any-*
> *thing to say? I read an amazing piece of writing yesterday,*
> *and I felt challenged to write more carefully, crafting each*
> *word, like I felt this author had done. This morning I just feel*
> *dull, uncreative, and empty. Father, why do I have such*
> *overwhelming doubts? I know that You have given me this*
> *opportunity to write, and I want to receive it with joy and*
> *confidence, but I don't feel joyful or confident. I'm tired and*
> *crabby, and I feel completely unworthy to write this book.*
> *Fresh-brewed life feels like an indictment rather than an invi-*
> *tation. I ask for Your presence . . .*

I started journaling when I was fifteen, on the day I became a Christian. My heart was full to overflowing, and there was no one to share it with but myself and God. I wanted to look at the words, savor the experience, feel the joy, and live every moment. I was so afraid I would forget what had happened to me.

I came to Christ on December 21, 1983, two days before my sixteenth birthday. My sister, Vanessa, was visiting with us over the Christmas holidays. She had been living with our dad, and we hadn't seen each other in a year or more. We had grown apart. She had given her life to Christ; I had given mine to drugs and alcohol.

We had stayed up late to talk. We were desperate to try to reconnect somehow since she had moved away, but we spoke different languages. I tried so hard to be cool and distant. But when Vanessa began talking about the love of Christ, God moved me. At that point her words ceased to be words, and I felt an earthquake in my soul. I didn't open my heart; I slowly cracked the door to peep out, and God tore the door off the hinges. His love entered my life like a raging river, and I was lost in a new way, in the intensity and passion of the greatest love I had ever known.

I have heard that it takes a new Christian about two years to forget what it was like to be without Christ. Hopelessness is replaced by arrogance. I didn't want to forget. My early journal writing was full of raw gratitude. I saw what God had saved me from: me. He had given me a chance to really live in the midst of death all around me. I would write these psalm-like odes of amazement and thankfulness in the evenings before I went to bed. At the close of my day I would pull out a blue cardboard-covered, spiral-bound notebook and pour my guts out on the page. My family was in shambles, and my journal became the first safe place I ever found to talk about the crazy world I lived in.

> "Whatever coaxes us out of hiding, to write, record, and express, is a revolutionary act. It says that we believe our lives count: our lives do count."
> —SARK

It was on those pages that I learned to bring my heart to God. I prayed in my journal. I cried as I wrote. I wondered out loud why things had happened the way they had. I asked God questions. I offered requests to God and then highlighted them when He answered. Journaling became for me the tangible representation of my relationship with God and others, and my wrestlings with the world around me. Fifteen years later, I still do the same things.

Countless other women journal as a way of life. This is Madeline L'Engle from *Walking on Water*:

> A help to me in working things out has been to keep an honest—as honest as the human being can be—unpublishable journal. Granted, much of my non-fiction work is lifted directly from my journals, but what I use is only a small fraction of these numerous, bulky volumes. If I can write things out I can see them, and they are not trapped within my own subjectivity. I have been keeping these notes of thoughts and questions and sometimes just garbage (which "needs" to be dumped somewhere) since I was about nine, I think, my free psychiatrist's couch.

Percolations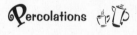

Books
Walking on Water, Madeline L'Engle
The Artist's Way, Julia Cameron
Inspiration Sandwich, SARK

Movies
The Color Purple
Out of Africa
The Shawshank Redemption

Growing

We have the opportunity to learn from life or to ignore its teaching. Most of us don't see the lessons because they are racing by us at the speed of life. We barely notice the passages of time. The school bus coming by for another pickup, the notches on your door-frame marking the kids' growth, the sunrise signaling another day, your haircut appointment reminding you six or eight weeks have flown by. We are not paying attention to our lives when we are merely reacting to the tasks required of us. When our souls ask deep questions, such as, *Are you making a difference?* We try to answer those questions with our "to do" list. "See," we say as we show our list, "we're getting a lot done."

Our lives have so much to teach us, and journaling gives us the opportunity to learn. By writing what's happening and what we are feeling, we can look at the pieces and study them. We can hear what our lives are saying to us, if nothing else, by the time or lack of time that we spend listening. When I open my journal and I haven't written in it for three weeks, that says more to me than someone telling me, "You're too busy." When I see that last entry and realize that I haven't commented on one sunset or written one reflection or talked back to anything I've read in three days, I am aware something must change.

In *Letters to Scattered Pilgrims*, Elizabeth O'Connor wrote,

Among our primary tools for growth are reflection, self-observation, and self-questioning. The journal is one of the most helpful vehicles we have for cultivating these great powers in ourselves. We all have these powers but we need structures that encourage us to use and practice them. Journal writing is enforced reflection. When we commit our observations to writing we are

Coffee is a fruit.

taking what is inside us and placing it outside us. We are holding a piece of our life in our hands where we can look at it, and meditate on it, and deepen our understanding of it.

Fresh-Brewed Adventures

- Take yourself on a creative date to find a journal. Don't rush! Look for a great pen and a small candle. Smell every candle until you find the right one. Get a cup of coffee, or tea, or hot chocolate after your purchases and sit at a table. Watch people and think about their lives. Then open your journal and make your first entry.
- Get up early in the morning before anyone gets up. Take your journal and your candle and find a quiet spot in your house. Read Psalm 130. Wait for the Lord. If He tells you something, write it down, and then do it.

Tasting

Living a fresh-brewed life isn't a spectator sport. It requires our participation. It is far easier to watch and observe life than it is to engage in it and enjoy it. Sometimes participating means that we buckle down and get our work done. We focus on the task at hand and give all of our available passion and energy to a job. But other times it means taking that drive with the sunroof open, playing our favorite CD, lying in the hammock with a glass of lemonade, or taking the kids where they want to go and playing like crazy. I love the MCI commercial about the stressed working mom who is racing around before work. She is stopped cold when her five-year-old daughter asks, "When can I be one of your clients?" She pauses, and says, "You've got five minutes to get ready for the beach, or I'm leaving without you." She doesn't blow off work completely, she just rearranges her schedule to taste her life a little bit more.

28

Tasting our lives. We spend more time telling ourselves why we can't do that than figuring out a way to do it. We rob ourselves of the joy that is already present in our lives simply by not taking advantage of the opportunities in front of us. This realization came from my journal, as I was accidentally tasting my life twice.

> *I had writing to do yesterday. I had self-imposed deadlines that I wanted to meet. I had lunch with friends outside on the deck of their home. We didn't hurry through the meal, or worry about the time. After lunch we pulled out a guitar and sang songs for a couple of hours. Around six, we loaded up the kids and we went to the beach and played. Boy, did we play. Two hours later, shoeless, wet, and covered with sand, we marched triumphantly back to our vehicles having played football and volleyball, and taken a quick swim. We tried to throw the Frisbee; I learned I can't throw a Frisbee; we did beach calisthenics, laughed at ourselves, and smiled until it was dark and we could barely see each other anymore. We stopped by the grocery and the movie place on the way home and spent the remainder of the evening eating coffee ice cream out of the carton, in our pajamas, in front of a complicated movie.*

> *I didn't write yesterday. I faced about thirty seconds of guilt last night before bed. I didn't write yesterday because I lived it.*

"We write to taste our life twice, in the moment and in retrospection."
—Anaïs Nin

Should I lock myself away to write about living a fresh-brewed life while that life is calling me to join it? Or should I trust that later I will have the opportunity to sit quietly with a smile still on my face, a bruise still on my arm from the volley-ball, sand still showing up in inconvenient places, and relive and record those memories? Not a tough call. I choose to live it first, and then taste it a second time when I write about it in my journal.

Your journal can remind you that you must make a life worth recording.

29

Observing

My journal is my constant companion. It is never very far from my reach. It goes to church with me; accompanies me on any excursion, fun, or work; it waits for me in the mornings beside my bed or on my desk; and it calls to me in the middle of a hectic day. It is a front porch of solace and retreat when I am tired and weary. It is a battleground of conflicting thoughts, each thought fighting to win the space. It is a stand-up comedy routine of witty, funny remarks. It is a newspaper column reporting the details of my life. It is a scrapbook collecting oddly shaped pieces of my experiences. And it is a monastery, where I seek to sit in the presence of God.

I write my thoughts on what's happening in my life. I write thoughts on what's happening in others' lives. Sometimes I write others' thoughts on what's happening in my life! The main thing is I'm writing, and when you are writing, you are thinking and feeling. You are processing, you are working things out. As you put words on the page, you know

> Better to write for yourself and have no public, than to write for the public and have no self.
> —Cyril Connolly

whether or not they represent you. You know when you are lying. You should say so immediately. I might write in the morning, "I'm tired, but I am looking forward to this day."

Then I think, *No I'm not. I'm being polite*. Then I write, "Why am I being polite in my journal? Who is going to read this? I don't have to be polite. I'm not looking forward to this day. I'm stressed, and this is one more thing that I feel I have to get finished before I can get on to what I want to do today." *There. I said it.* "Why do I feel so stressed today? Because I said yes to Karen, when I should have said no. I was trying to be polite again. Okay: Big RED flag . . . you are too polite." I sit with that big red flag for a minute and think about "too polite." I continue writing, "That doesn't mean too kind or too considerate of others. Politeness for me can have an outward appearance of kindness without really being kind. Yuck! I am spending way too much time and energy trying to please everyone else."

> "People would ask what I did, and I would say, 'I'm a writer!' They inevitably would ask, 'What do you write?'
> "When I answered 'journals,' sometimes they chuckled or smirked, as though journals were less valuable somehow."
>
> —SARK

I discover things when I write in my journal. How else can we learn about ourselves if not by forcing our hands to tell the truths of our hearts? Some people hold back in their journals, thinking that someone will read it. They write more spiritually than they live, and they don't tell the truth about where they are. One friend made the observation that not being honest in your journal is like trying to cheat on your own health exam!

The grass in the front yard is brown. It's been too long since the last rain. The consistency of that big fat star is astounding and maddening. It rises every day, and it burns all day long. Without rain, there is no way for the grass to survive this constant baking. I am brown, spotted, and parched. The sun of this trial, and two weeks with not one drop of rain have left me scorched and hard. I am angry and hot. My soul cries out for water in this arid place. God, bring rain soon. To the grass in my front yard, and to the grass in my soul. I won't make it without You.

31

In an *Image* magazine article, Elizabeth Dewberry wrote, "The artist therefore has to be willing to go into that place in her soul which is so deep and so dark that she can't see her way around, where she can't rely on traditional knowledge or conventional ways of knowing, and she has to open her eyes to whatever's there. That is in itself an act of faith."

Recipes

Cappuccino: One shot of espresso with one shot of steamed milk.
Café Latte: One shot of espresso with two shots of steamed milk.

Starting

Some of you have been journaling for years, and it is as comfortable to you as your slippers in the evening. But for others this will be a new process. Maybe you have journaled off and on and have never been able to stick with it with any consistency. Don't give up, but don't beat yourself up either. The worst thing that you can do is to try to make some new commitment that you won't be able to live up to. Relax. Keeping a journal should never be a pressure; it is an invitation to an oasis, like a quiet time with God. People don't say, "I'm so thirsty. I guess I have to drink water today. Just one more thing to do." They run to the water.

An Inviting Journal

Search for a journal that is right for you. Certain things will "work" for you as you try out a journal or two. Some like lines and others like no lines. You might like spiral-bound or more book-style. None of the features of your journal matter except that you like them. Your journal needs to inspire you to pick it up; it should beg to be written in. I love beautiful artwork or creative wording on my journals. When I find a good journal, every time I look at it, my heart jumps a little. I feel a sense of connection with the pages. I feel that writing in such a book will change me in some way. I also like to feel as though it can hold my life. I prefer thick pages that have some weight and texture to them, but I have written in journals that have thin, fragile paper. Believe it or not, my writing is affected by the kind of paper I write on. It's fun to experiment and see what kind best draws out your words.

An Exclusive Pen

I love pens, markers, colored pencils, crayons, and all things writeable. Marking in your journal with lipstick is permissible (and encouraged), but a favorite pen for your journal is a must. Be careful when you write with a pencil, that you not give in to your temptation to erase. In your journal you want to keep all the words, even if you think they are the wrong ones. Search for a pen that is fun to write with and feels comfortable in your hand. I like pens whose ink flows freely and evenly, so it doesn't slow down my writing. I learned early that ink that doesn't dry quickly can make a mess when you're writing fast and your hand is gliding over the page. A good pen is a great investment. Keep it with your journal. Always use it only for your journal so it is there when you need it, at a moment's notice. That way, your great idea or revelation or invention that changes the world won't leave you before you find a pen.

A Window of Time

Time to journal is essential, but don't neglect journaling even if you don't have a large chunk of time to devote to it. Sometimes you can take five minutes and get two thoughts down that will affect the rest of your day. However, when you have some time, spend it with your journal writing and don't rush. It is not a waste of your time. Switch off "productivity mode" and realize that you are investing in your growth. And that takes slow, steady steps. Seeking to savor your life through words is never a frivolous use of your time. The house will still be falling down around you when you get done, but you will have a new peace about how to put it back together.

33

A Comfy Place

I don't always get to "create a space" for journaling, but I always try. Sometimes I will light a candle and put a CD on. Other times I will curl up by the window with a cup of coffee. One of my favorite things to do is sit outside on our deck or take my journal to the hammock. I am always seeking to create an environment where my soul feels relaxed. I try to make sure that it is relatively free of distraction. Sometimes the bathroom is your only option; I understand that. It's okay to journal in the bathroom. Or you can take the tactic of Susanna Wesley (mother of Charles and John and fifteen others): throw a sheet over your head and sit in the corner! (I think throwing the sheet over the kitchen table and getting under it would give you more room. And you could light a candle!) Any way you can, create a space that invites you to join it. A special atmosphere is a great way to set the mood for your writing.

Complete Candor

When you begin to write your thoughts and feelings, you shouldn't be saying to yourself, *I can't write that*. That becomes

Coffee beans aren't beans; they are berries (often called cherries) and they're green.

34

the very thing you must write. You have to silence the critic inside you that will critique your writing or shut down your feelings. After you have written a sentence, resist the urge to go back and read it. Just keep writing; don't interrupt the flow. If you look again at your words, you will pick them apart or dismiss them or want to rewrite them. Don't give in to this. Your job is to get honest words and feelings down on the paper, not justify them or explain them or make sure they are beautiful: vomit on paper; explode with excitement; weep; laugh as you relive the memories; plod through the humdrum details of your day; scream at the pages; press hard with your pen; write honestly.

Personal Privacy

Will you write what you really feel if you know others might read it? My journal is off-limits to anyone but me. It isn't a book to be read by others. It is not for anyone else's reading. I can't wrestle on paper if I fear what someone else might think of my wrestling. That's when we end up writing things like, "I know I shouldn't feel this way . . ." or we paste a conclusion on our writing that we don't believe like, "I guess that God is going to work this out . . ." but inside we don't trust at all.

In fact, if you must keep your journal hidden, do so. I feel so sad for women or men who can't write from their hearts without fear that their spouses or families will read what they have written. Why would it be a secret, why shouldn't your spouse be able to read your journal? Because they are your thoughts and your feelings. Your wrestlings. If you are only writing things that are appropriate for others to read, you probably aren't wrestling deep enough. You are always free to share thoughts from your journal, and on some occasions you might invite someone else to read a passage, but it should never be expected or demanded. It's a matter of trust that should never be violated. If you do violate that trust and read someone else's private writing, you deserve what you get. We all need a safe, hidden place to reveal our doubts, fears, and wrestlings. How can we bring them to God otherwise? We all struggle with our humanity, and if you haven't yet, hopefully you will by the time you finish this book. There is no short-cut to dealing with our fallenness. If we say we have no sin, we deceive ourselves and the truth

> "Satisfy us in the morning with your unfailing love,
> that we may sing for joy and be glad all our days."
> —Psalm 90:14

is not in us (1 John 1:8). Our journals become holy means to express our lives as we reveal our sin, our hopes, our longings, our shortcomings, our triumphs. Sometimes my journal entries are just long prayers to God, and I write "Amen" at the end. In private.

Spiritual Direction

I like to have my Bible with me or nearby while I'm journaling. I usually read a passage of Scripture in the morning, and often my first journal thoughts are remarks or responses to what I have just read. My writing is dialogue with what I'm reading. If something speaks to me deeply, it goes in the journal. Sometimes the Lord will direct me to a familiar passage like Psalm 23 just to remind me of the still waters that He offers. My Bible is right there for me to find whatever passage He might direct me to. I can then hear Him and respond.

Encountering God

Journaling is not just about writing. It is also about listening. As you have your journal open, write as fast as your hand will go, and listen. But not to your internal editor. If

36

something in your head says *Don't write that down,* or *You shouldn't feel that way,* that's editing. You have to press through that distraction, or you will never get anywhere. But when you are writing and you hear the voice of love, let it stop you, and listen. When you are pouring your heart out or putting down thoughts about a psalm, keep the ears of your spirit open for the voice of God. God speaks to me more when I have my journal out and my heart open than any other time in the day.

Journaling isn't just the writing and recording of our activities, it can also be the handwriting of God, if we will allow Him the freedom to write into our lives. When we are struggling, He will meet us on the pages. When we are sinning, He will reveal that to us. When we are weeping, we'll hear His gentle words of comfort. And when we write in celebration, we can hear His shouts of joy coming through our own.

So this morning, or the next time you get your journal out, just sit with it for a few minutes. Think about an area of your life that needs God's guidance. Maybe it's money, perhaps a friendship, even your spiritual journey. Pray a very simple prayer like, "Lord, I am listening, please speak to me," and then write down what He tells you. You may not hear anything immediately. Just be patient, and wait. You may hear so much that you can't write fast enough. Either way, listen, and then write. Jeannie Miley calls this the art of creative silence. Use the silence to listen to God, even if He doesn't seem to be speaking. Sometimes it takes our hearts a while to learn to hear Him. Keep your Bible handy, not forgetting that He has spoken and still speaks through His Word. Sometimes His answer to you will be a Scripture verse. Sometimes in the middle of a struggle He will direct you to an appropriate passage. Just keep listening.

Coffee contains twice as much caffeine as tea.

The Coffee Song

I'm watching life around me and wishing it were mine,
Making up the stories with the pieces that I find.
Why is that man laughing,
And who is she thinking of,
And where were those two when they met
And when they fell in love . . .

So I pour another cup and watch the steam dance in the air,
I dream about where I will be tomorrow and wish that I was
already there.

An hour passed, time goes so fast,
Why can't we just stand still?
And the coffee that I'm drinking is much stronger than my will.
I spent the morning mourning chances I could never take,
Now I've got some time to think, and I think the afternoon can
wait . . .

So I pour another cup and watch the steam dance in the air,
I dream about where I will be tomorrow and wish that I was
already there.

—1997 Manor Music

Encountering Opposition

I hear voices in my head all day long. I've talked to a lot of
other women who do, too, so I know I'm not completely alone
here. Although, I do feel a bit like Ray Kinsella in *Field of
Dreams*. When he said out loud that he was hearing voices, the
rumors began to fly, the heads began to shake, "Ray is hearing
voices in the cornfield." Well, so be it. But my voice isn't calling

me to build. The voice I hear tears me down. It rises up in me to create fear or to try to convince me that I don't have value. I can be minding my own business, cleaning up the kitchen, and from out of nowhere a voice will tell me, *You don't know how to keep a clean house.* Or, when I sit down to write, the voice nags me, *You don't have anything to say. No one wants to listen to you.*

You're too fat!

Who do you think you are?

You can't do that.

Nothing ever changes.

You say you will, but you won't.

You can't ever say no to chocolate.

If people really knew you . . .

You think you're making a difference, but you're not.

Why are you doing that? Nobody cares anyway.

You don't have your own life under control, so how can you tell others anything?

These voices keep our souls chained in the basement. They make us fearful to try anything new, anxious about what others think of us, and they keep us on the treadmill of performance. In short, if we allow them, these voices can easily rob every ounce of enjoyment from the lives we have. Many women don't even know they are giving power to the voices, living in a state of constant self-disapproval. Understand this: these voices can immobilize us and keep us from dreaming our dreams. They can discourage us and cause us to think too small and expect too little from our lives. Or they can yell and demand that we expect more from our lives and beat us up for not "doing more." They make us afraid to be who we are. The voices can keep us from writing books or changing careers or loving our children well.

But only if we let them.

Journaling and listening to God are the only ways I have

The average American adult consumes 26.7 gallons of coffee per year.

found to ferret out those voices and loosen their devastating power over me. I want to be crystal clear: the voices we hear in our heads are not from God.

Your journaling in the morning will bring out these voices with a vengeance. As you begin to write about your longings and put your hopes on paper, just get ready for the peanut gallery. Whenever a woman seeks to move courageously in her world, clothed in passion and humility, the enemy of her soul is going to move against her.

Let me encourage you, my sister, press forward. Write it all down. Somehow when I write what the voices say, it is easier to deal with them. When I pen the words, *You don't have worth, your thighs are too big!* I can look at those words and see them for what they are—a fear tactic from the hater of my life— and then I can let them go. Most of the time. And it's far easier when I am looking at the words written on the page than when I am staring at the ceiling at two in the morning, terrified by them. To write about them is to take the sting out and drag them into the light where they cannot survive. I have often written down what I'm hearing in my head, and it ends up next to something I have heard from God, and the contrast is astounding. As I am looking at the page, it becomes clear that I have a choice of whom to side with.

Directed Journaling

- What keeps you from tasting your life?
- Write down things you always hear "the voices" say. Who said that to you first?
- Imagine yourself completely surrendering to God. How different would your life look?

Encountering Creativity

40

Writing has awakened an avenue of creativity for me. I first strolled down that avenue through journaling, and a new creative world opened up. I could see shops, restaurants, art galleries, and pet stores, where before there was nothing. Piquing my curiosity, this street made me wonder if there were more roads like these. My writing time in the morning became an adventure into unfamiliar towns.

God is the Author of creativity. As we turn down the volume on the destructive voices, we are free to turn up the creativity. We cannot write freely or creatively, in our journals or otherwise, when we are constantly criticizing ourselves. And there is more to life. It's time to explore and dream, imagine and play. God is the quintessential Creator, and we are created in His image. It pleases Him when we create. "In the beginning," means before there was anything. He flung the stars into a space where there was nothing. We are like God when we create something from nothing. When there is a blank page and we fill it with words, or an empty canvas and we heap color on it, or an empty refrigerator and we stock it with food for wonderful meals—we are creating something where in the beginning there was nothing. Granted, creating meatloaf is not quite like creating mankind, but . . . originality reveals our heavenly DNA.

> "Writing is easy: all you have to do is sit staring at the blank sheet of paper until the drops of blood form on your forehead."
> —Gene Fowler

Consider, then, that we are like our adversary when we are imitators. When we eliminate our own creativity merely to copy someone else, I'm not sure that we are reflecting God. Creativity is hard. On the seventh day, God didn't rest because He was tired, but sometimes we are. We aren't God, so creativity, or any kind of work, takes a toll on us. Staring down at a blank piece of paper is tough, and sometimes the paper wins. When fear gets the best of us, we settle for imitation.

I challenge you, as I challenge myself, to let your God-given creativity surface. The world needs you. The church needs you. We need your ideas, your insights, your colors, your contribution. What you are passionate about was created in you to make a splash in this life that no one else can make. Make it. Make it now.

Encountering a journal is the cup of fresh-brewed life that woke me up to creativity. It is also the cup that keeps me awake to God and to myself. Without it, I wouldn't be tasting my life, or reflecting on my journey or writing this book. A journal is a tool, a flower, a canvas, a safety deposit box, a cup of coffee with a friend. It can hold your dreams, record your life, challenge your thinking, refresh your soul, tickle your sides, and redirect your steps. That is, if you bring your whole-bean self to the encounter. If you haven't yet started journaling, you're in for a satisfying surprise as the warmth of this cup presses against your lips. If you're an old pro, you already know how important this is. I encourage you, just keep drinking.

Three

LISTEN TO YOUR LONGINGS

Staring out the sliding glass door into the ocean, a strong sense of emptiness fills her heart. It is her last day of vacation. She doesn't hate her life or her job, yet the thought of returning to both causes great sadness. She'll be at her desk tomorrow, waiting another year for vacation. An ache sets in. She was made for more.

Patty wipes a tear as she hangs up the phone. It is always so hard to say good-bye. Her best friend lives ten hours away, and the loneliness she feels is from more than just the miles separating them. They are soul mates, and Patty yearns for more time together. They had just spent an hour on the phone and could easily have spent more. "What is wrong with me? Why can't I be grateful for the time we have instead of being depressed that we don't have more?" She can't muster up the gratitude, and she puts her head in her hands and weeps. She was made for more.

They have been married for fifteen years. They are still in love and deeply committed to each other. But they are different, and as much as she doesn't want to admit it, there

44

are times when Caroline finds empty places in her soul that Jack can't reach. She tries not to think about it much, she stays really busy, but there are times when she feels like a complete stranger to him. Does he really know me? *she wonders as she lies awake at night.* Do I really know me? *The next morning as she washes her hair, she tries to send the feelings right down the drain with the shampoo. She was made for more.*

Longings. Coming face-to-face with the fact that there are empty places in our lives that haven't been filled. Yearnings. Wanting more than we have: more love, more enjoyment, more passion, more hope, more rest. Cravings. The hope of finding something that will satisfy the rumbling we feel in the stomach of our soul.

Longings can begin to surface after a number of years in the same job. Women begin to wonder, "Is this all there is?" The same awakening happens in a marriage when a woman realizes that she wants more love or tenderness than her husband can give. At the dinner table in the middle of supper, a hope for peace and a yearning for rest begin to rise up.

You were made for more than this world has to offer you.

Our yearnings, longings, cravings, and hopes are telling us something: there isn't enough love, peace, hope, friendship, and intimacy on this earth to completely satisfy us. We will always want more.

That's why we can have a marvelous vacation that satisfies us deeply on one level and leaves us empty on another. That's why we can receive praise and honor from other people and yet feel insecure and alone at the same time. We were made to run on high-test fuel, and the best we get here is 89-grade octane. It's not that we are ungrateful or greedy. God has designed us to want more out of life, and we won't be satisfied until we get it. We cry out to God over this, "How long must I wait, O Lord?" Still we are left longing.

This feels like a no-win situation. Are longings one big cosmic setup for frustration? Perhaps, if we view them as something to be overcome or eradicated. If we spend more time trying to get them "filled up." But if we lean in close, and put our ears to the chest of our soul and listen to our longings— they can teach us to understand God and ourselves in a way that would not happen if we were permitted to have everything we longed for. It's true, what we don't have shapes us more than what we have. We are like Swiss cheese, and the holes in us are actually *supposed* to be there. The holes are the things that make us who we are. The holes are the places God has reserved in us for Himself! The longings identify our real hunger. A hunger that drives us to Him to be satisfied. *If* . . . big *if* . . . we listen.

For whatever reason, this has been the year I have awakened to longing. I am looking at my own personal yearnings, desires, wishes: those places in my soul that feel hollow and empty and unsatisfied. I can't lie and say it has been great. It has brought pain and sadness in some areas. But I can say with honesty that allowing myself to listen to my longings, rather than running from them, has radically changed me. Finding the courage to stare into the caverns of my own soul has fostered a dependency on God that I have not known before. Therein lies the treasure we seek. Longings are the map that will point the way.

"Now wait a minute, Nicole," you may be saying. "I signed on for a fresh-brewed life, not the staring-into-the-caverns-of-my-soul thing. It's dark in there. I'm looking for the light. I want the joy, the excitement, the completeness, the wake-up call. You are talking about pain and unfulfillment."

I haven't pulled a bait and switch, I promise. A fresh-brewed life will never mean the absence of pain. What it means is the presence of life. There is no life without pain. No treasure without the hunt. How I wish that weren't so. Getting things easily will never make us into the women God is calling us to be. Let's wake up and investigate the caverns. Our longings have so much to tell us.

Wishes, Dreams, and Longings

A longing is an intense desire for something that is out of our reach. A dream is a strong desire for something that could be within our reach. Dreams and longings are like mothers and daughters—different, but related. Wishes are wants and desires. They're still in the same family with longings and dreams, but they are more like first cousins. They're more common and attainable. Though they're sometimes used interchangeably, longings, dreams, and wishes are distinctly separate. If we confuse them, we could find ourselves depressed very easily. Say we are *dreaming* of something (remember a dream could be within our reach), like a perfect husband. Actually, that is not a dream at all, but a longing, and we are going to be in a bad place if we confuse the two. We'll be waiting a long time for that perfect husband, and we'll be awfully disappointed during the waiting.

Here's the difference:

You wish for a relationship
you dream of a husband
you long for a perfect man.

You wish for some cash
you dream of more money
you long for enough money to take away all your problems.

You wish for more time

you dream of an incredible vacation
you long for a place of complete freedom and rest.

You wish to be thinner
you dream of being a size four
you long to be Gwyneth Paltrow.

All of them, wishes, dreams, and longings, have something to tell us. Each of them points the way to the treasure we are seeking. But the same road that leads to the treasure is full of deep potholes of disappointment.

℘ercolations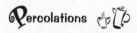

Books

Yearning, Craig Barnes
When the Heart Waits, Sue Monk Kidd

Movies

City of Angels
Trip to Bountiful
The Horse Whisperer

Music

Big Horizon, David Wilcox
Flyer, Nancy Griffith
Behind the Eyes, Amy Grant

Two Ways We Try to "Manage" Disappointment

When it happens is different for everyone, but you know when you've hit a pothole—the realization that you are not going to get all that you long for in this world. You look at your life and your relationships, and you feel a nagging sense of, *Is this all there is?* Deep disappointment. These feelings are the precursors to waking up to our longings. They are the first stirrings of understanding that we were made for more. But unfortunately, when we have these feelings we usually run in one of two directions.

The first direction we take is to become "spectators" *watching* our own lives. We refuse to fully participate. We become conscientious objectors to real life. It's the turtle approach. We stay busy, but we keep all the vital stuff inside the shell. We never pause long enough to listen to our dreams, so we don't have to be responsible to them. Let's face it—it works for us. If we don't wish or dream, we aren't disappointed. If we aren't disappointed, we can tolerate our lives. We settle for toleration because we gave up on enjoyment a long time ago, when disappointment started to creep in. We don't allow ourselves to even *wonder* what it would be like to plant a garden, volunteer at a hospice, take up watercolors, go to cooking school, earn a master's degree, sing in a quartet, write a book, run a race. *There isn't time. I couldn't possibly. Why entertain the thoughts? They only lead to constant disappointment.*

> "O God, You are my God, / earnestly I seek you; / my soul thirsts for you, / my body longs for you, / in a dry and weary land / where there is no water."
> —Psalm 63:1

Even if you become android woman, you can't completely kill your soul. Dreams and longings have a way of resurfacing. We are flipping through a magazine and see an amazing garden. Something washes over us. We ignore it. A friend reveals a painting that she finished, and you find yourself jealous. *Where did that feeling come from?* You've never been a jealous person. You start thinking, *I could have done that . . . I wish I had done that.* You're watching a movie about Africa, and a

48

powerful yearning stirs in your soul to visit there. It starts a chain reaction of places flashing through your mind. *Paris, Australia, San Francisco.* Places you have always wanted to visit. Only this time as those places surface in your mind, you can't see yourself ever going. Now you can't stop the tears. It only takes a moment before you try to squelch the sadness. *Stop crying,* you think, *some things are just never meant to be. I can't expect too much out of life.* The spectators see disappointment as something wrong with *them.*

The second tactic we employ to deal with our disappointment is to become "evaluators" *criticizing* our lives. We rise above living life to judging life and the quality of everything. We look as if we are participating, but we stay quite removed from any real experience. We are "sampling" and evaluating, operating like critics in life. You never ask a movie critic or a food reviewer, "Did you like it?" That would bring stern disapproval. The goal is not to like a movie or enjoy a meal; the goal is to evaluate it based on its merit and ability, which you determine based on its potential to bring satisfaction to you or others. And satisfaction is something we know we can't have, so we pick everything apart. We move in worlds of pleasure but find very little. We deny ourselves nothing and still miss contentment. We hear about a new "whatever," and we know that it will be

> "Jealousy is an oddly wrapped gift that points the way toward where we want to go."
> —SARK

ours. We buy things to dismiss them. *That didn't make me happy* . . . We are on a constant search to find the ultimate experience that will vanquish disappointment from our lives.

Even if you become a critical snob, you can't completely kill your soul. Dreams and longings have a way of resurfacing. Simple, unexpected things, like joy, surprise you in the middle of a family gathering. *Where did that come from? These people don't understand anything about life.* Yet you find yourself laughing and connecting with them. You're shopping and you decide *not* to buy something, and you go home feeling a little different, hopeful somehow that there is more to life than "stuff." You're getting a massage and you wonder what it would be like to sell your big house and move out into the country. *How would that ever satisfy me?* You begin to wonder if you've "missed life" somehow. Even the evaluator sheds a few tears, but quickly criticizes herself. *Stop crying and get over it. Head back to that new store that opened up next to the art gallery.* And you set out to find a new "drug" to eliminate the disappointment so you can be back to your old, critical self in no time. The evaluators see disappointment as something wrong with *life*.

We are masters at killing our own dreams, one way or another. We extinguish the flame of possibility before anyone else has the opportunity to blow it out. It really is safer that way. Because what if we really stumble onto things that we want and there's no way we can have them? What would we do with that? If you said to your husband over dinner, "I was thinking about going back to school," and he made fun of the idea or rejected the notion, what would that say to your soul? I mean, taking up watercolors is one thing, but what about deeper desires? Cooking classes would be fun, but it won't satisfy your dream of having a better marriage. What if you wanted to sell your house and move to a mission area in Africa? Quick, douse the flame before you get burned.

Neither spectators nor evaluators are living a fresh-brewed life. Trying to sidestep disappointment doesn't bring the satisfaction that we think it will. Avoiding pain isn't synonymous with embracing life. We need to become "participators," *engaging our lives*. That means we are on the field playing, not in the stands watching, or on the sidelines criticizing. The participator is the one who listens to her dreams, pencil in hand, to learn from them. *Why do I feel this drive to go back to school? What do I really want? Maybe I could sell the house. Is it too important to me?* The participator faces disappointment head-on, recognizing it to be part of life, that pain comes from living in a broken world. She knows she won't have everything she wants, but that doesn't make her pull in the sign and close up shop.

We also move to spectate or evaluate because we are afraid of pain.

Pain and Fear

"I want morphine." I walked in and told them so. Loudly. I had another kidney stone, and I wanted to get started on heavy drugs as soon as possible. "I'm sorry, Mrs. Johnson, but before we can give you medication, we have to admit you to the hospital." Details. I knew the pain that was around the corner if I didn't get medicine fast. I didn't want to wait. Hospitals have these inane rules about dispensing medication, like, they have to diagnose the problem before they give you any. I guess it's a silly little precaution that keeps them from treating you for something that you don't really have, or from giving you medicine that could actually hurt you. But when you are in pain, you don't care if they give you Drano as long as it will bring some kind of relief. Knock me out, take the edge off, send me to la-la land—anything—just make the pain go away.

We don't want to listen to our longings. We don't like them. We don't want them. When you want something that you cannot have, it isn't pleasant. If you agree to be honest about what you want in your life, it can be downright painful. Longings are inconvenient, uncomfortable, embarrassing at best; uncontrollable, revealing, terrifying, and potentially devastating at worst. They cause us pain and fear. They interrupt our lives with their nagging and persistence and keep us from feeling contented with what we have. We worry that they are assassins of our faith and betrayals of our loved ones.

I want to run away from home, I want my kids to run away from home, I want to eat every last cookie in the world, I want to be Miss America, I want to take a nap, I want to live at the beach, I want to write a best-selling book, I want cellulite-free thighs, I want a beautiful house, I want more passion in my marriage, I want a soul mate friend, I want . . .

This scares us to death.

We are afraid of our longings. We're afraid if we say we want to eat cookies that we'll eat two boxes and never stop. Or if we cry out for more passion in our marriage, then we are going to have an affair. Or if we desire something like beauty then we must not be Christian enough. We are afraid that if we give ourselves permission to confess our longing, fear will tell us there is no turning back and we're inevitably going to pursue whatever we think will satisfy it. So instead of naming our longings and listening to what they would tell us, we try to cut them off. "Get back to work," or "Face facts," we say to our souls.

But longings are part of being alive. When we try to cut them off, we are trying to keep ourselves safe from life. Longings challenge us to be more than evaluators or spectators; they call us to be participators in our very short existence.

> "When at last I cling to you with all my being, for me there will be no more sorrow, no more toil. Then at last I shall be alive with true life, for my life will be wholly filled by you."
>
> —Saint Augustine

At this point, some people would say, "Die to yourself!" That is the *Christian* thing to do. Christians have all sorts of "spiritual" strategies for dealing with fear and pain. Don't miss my point: we do have to die to ourselves, and that is what the Christian life is about, but you have to *live* in order to *die*. Women want to go straight to "die to yourself" before they even know what self they are dying to. Then it is not a laying down of their lives, but a complete avoidance of pain. That, my friend, is seeking to *save* your life, which is something different altogether. God does not intend us to cut off our longings or live in fear of them. He gave them to us. They call us to Him.

This is permission to start naming your longings. Write them down. It is important that you identify what you are longing for, so you can listen to what it means. It's like discovering what you're hungry for *before* you start eating. You are not giving yourself permission to try to foolishly meet your longings, you are simply naming them, and seeking to understand their message.

To wake up to the truth that you were made for more than this world has to offer will change your life. When you are honest about the places in your soul that ache to be filled, you are right where God can tenderly reach in and touch the deepest parts of your heart.

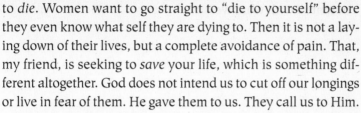

Directed Journaling

- What are you jealous of?
- What is someone else doing that you wish you were doing?
- Write about two longings in your life.
- What do you dream about?

The Longing of God

Here is an amazing truth: God has longings too. Although God is perfect, complete, whole, omnipotent, omni-everything, He still longs for one thing: us. This blows me away. He set up

His own universe to potentially leave Himself unfulfilled. God's desire is that none should perish, yet He gave us the freedom to choose Him as the path to salvation. When we don't choose Him, He is not getting what He wants. He is left longing.

Not only is God left longing when we don't respond to Him as our Savior, but His longing and grief are very much in the now whenever we place our idols before our relationship with Him. He seeks a love relationship with us, and our choice to direct our passion elsewhere leaves our Creator longing.

When we cry out in the midst of our unmet needs, we are in good company. The best company in the universe. We are free to bring our longings to Him who is intimately acquainted with long-ings, our heavenly Father. He placed Adam and Eve in the garden, and even before there was sin, there were boundaries. The Tree of Life was off-limits for them. They knew longing before they knew sin. Our longings are not sinful. The lengths we might go to in our efforts to meet them could be, but the longings themselves are not. Can you imagine if Eve had gone to God when she was tempted by the snake? What if she had wept and said, "I was tempted, I wanted so badly to eat of the fruit You told me not to eat." Do you think God would have punished her? Or would He have put His arms around her and held her close? Our longings have the power to draw us to God in a passionate, desperate way that nothing else can.

> "The tragedy of life is not in the fact of death, but in what dies inside us while we live."
> —Norman Cousins

There are areas in my life that I cannot get filled outside of God. I can do some temporary filling, but not the kind my soul craves. The longing to be filled, the longing to be known, and the longing for heaven all draw me to Him with an intense pull that began the day He made me.

The Longing to Be Filled

I am slow, but thirty-two years of this pattern are sinking in. I have a longing to be filled, and I try unsuccessfully to sate it with food, purchases, and even people. Every time I go to the mall, a million things jump out at me that I want to buy, and the tempter promises me that if I max out my card with awesome purchases then I will feel fulfilled. It feels great for a while, but then the bill comes and the longing has come back with it. What am I trying to sate at every meal or with each purchase that is monumentally bigger than wanting French fries or new place mats? My deep, powerful longing to be filled.

This longing rears its head in my life at the table, at the mall, and at the mirror. This is the longing to not have longings. When I eat too much or buy too much or obsess about the way I look, I am trying to fill up my longing for wholeness. I want to have all I need and more. I don't want to feel empty or lacking or less than perfect.

Physical food is a need of course; we have to have it for nutrition. But food is also about enjoyment, which makes a Snickers bar a wish, a desire, a want. A $250 dinner at The French Laundry in Yountville, California, is a dream. It's possible, but it won't happen often. But the craving to be completely filled, whole, perfect, and satisfied is a longing. I don't want enough; I want more than enough. I don't want to eat just until I "feel" full, I want to make sure I am full. I want to be in charge of my own filling and not stop until I say "when." Something inside me promises satisfaction if I eat large quantities of chocolate. So I do. For a short time I do feel some satisfaction. Until I'm fatter. Then the longing returns, and I feel duped. Why? Because all along it's not a longing for chocolate; it's so much deeper than that. Sometimes, when the desire to feel filled kicks in strongly, I have to say out loud, "This is not a longing for chocolate." Then people wonder who I am talking to.

56

Emotionally, in relationships we do the same thing. What we do to try to meet this longing would be comical if it weren't so destructive. Have you noticed that the law of diminishing returns applies in relationships just like when you sit down to a meal or go shopping? The more you get, the more you want, and the less satisfied you feel. Have you ever had this conversation?*

WOMAN: Honey, do you like this dress?
MAN: Uh, hunh.
WOMAN: Is that a yes?
MAN: Yes.
WOMAN: Then why didn't you say yes?
MAN: I did.
WOMAN: No you didn't; you said, uh, hunh.
MAN: That means yes.
WOMAN: Not to me.
MAN: What means yes to you?
WOMAN: The word *yes.*
MAN: Give me another chance.
WOMAN: Do you like this dress?
MAN: Yes.
WOMAN: Now you're just saying that.
(*Excerpted here from my own marriage for your enjoyment.)

Why do we engage in this kind of emotional dance? This is not a superficial conversation about a dress; it is a strategy women employ to get emotionally filled. Wanting to be full is a legitimate longing, but seeking to meet that longing by manipulating another person to fill it is sinful.

The Longing to Be Known
Meg Ryan takes a bite out of a pear.

"What does it taste like?" Nicolas Cage asks her in *City of Angels*.

She laughs. "Don't you know what a pear tastes like?"

"Yes, but I don't know what a pear tastes like *to you*."

Every woman in the theater melts, including me.

As much as we conceal and cover up, women long to be uncovered, discovered, and known. As much as we run and hide, we have a far deeper longing to be found. Every woman on the face of the earth wants to be pursued and embraced passionately. What an incredibly strong longing! This is the one that drives us to romance novels and soap operas. I am willing to admit I've watched *General Hospital,* and I've read my share of trashy novels, but let's face it, these stir up our longings but they don't come anywhere close to meeting them. I mean, they are written by women! No one knows how to identify a woman's longings like another woman. Women can create men who will speak our language and meet every need. But, these men don't exist. That's not to say there aren't wonderful godly men out there—there are, but they are still going to fall short.

> "There are two sources of unhappiness in life. One is not getting what you want; the other is getting it."
> —George Bernard Shaw

Even Billy Graham cannot meet his wife's every need. So I feel set up by those romance writers. They cast men in a role only God can fill, and it's no wonder we come away disappointed in our husbands.

So, unless you can get your husband or boyfriend to read to you out of one of these books or say the lines from a great movie, you're out of luck. Even if you can get him to say them, it won't work because he'll say them wrong. I told my husband, Paul, about the lines in *City of Angels* and he said, "I didn't know you liked pears."

Like Caroline at the beginning of this chapter, there are

places in you that your relationships don't touch. If you're a woman, this is the case. You're going to have to face to some degree your unmet longing to be known. I am married to a fabulous man. I am convinced that he is who God intended for me, and I love him but I still weep over this longing. Because no matter how much he knows me, there is still more to know, more to be embraced. So the yearning continues and it calls me to look upward.

It is really easy to get angry with men about this. Why can't they be all that we want them to be? Why can't they meet our every longing? Unfortunately, God placed the same limitations on men that He did on us. It's quite a heavy realization for men when they begin to see that they can't fill all the empty places inside their wives. They can't run to Home Depot for that one. While they can know us, and while we can have *incredibly* satisfying relationships, they will never be all that we long for.

The Longing for Heaven

I usually don't spend much time thinking about heaven. In fact, when this longing for heaven surfaced, it was a surprise to me. Heaven, to me, was just the wonderful place we go when we die. It didn't dawn on me that we came from heaven and that we would feel a homesickness in our souls until we return.

For when all is said and done, there is only this to say: No matter how sweet the event, how consoling the moment, there is always a deep longing within us that cuts like a knife. It is a yearning that stirs even when (or perhaps most often when) the air is flooded with sunshine and the sky dazzles us with color and light. Then this unutterable loneliness that we feel is in no way justified. Yet in the midst of our grat-

itude for the beauty of created things, we know in our very bones that there is something yet to be given. The emptiness is the mark and reminder of God. By this sense of what is not, we know what is and what is yet to be.

59

Paul and I went to South Africa for our tenth anniversary. I was not prepared for the onslaught of longing that was awakened within me. Never have I so deeply connected with a physical place on the globe. Travel has always been something I enjoyed, but usually by the end of a trip I am ready to go home. Not so with Africa. "This country has stalked and captured my wandering heart," I wrote in my journal. I never had so many thoughts about running away from home and living in another land. It wasn't just the sheer beauty of this country, it was a combination of everything—the amazing animals, the relationships we built while there, the aliveness I felt in my soul just waking up in Africa.

I couldn't see this yearning while I was there and enjoying the country, but I began to taste the longing about three days before we had to leave. It knocked on my door, and I was afraid to answer. On the flight home, I opened the door, and an overwhelming longing flooded my soul.

I want to live in a place with animals. I want to feel the wildness of life all around me. I want to be free from faxes and phones and electronic communication. I want to sit

"So when I feel lonely, I know that is only a sign some room is empty, that room is there by design and when I feel hollow that's just my proof that there's more for me to follow—that's what the lonely is for."

—David Wilcox, "That's What the Lonely Is For"

around a big table and enjoy fellowship with people from all over the world. At the end of the day, when the cooling begins,

60

I want to breathe in the clean air of a simpler earth. I want heaven. And on earth I'm not going to get any more than a taste of that, and that makes me ache.

The Ultimate Longing: The Treasure

The writer in Psalm 42 cried out, "As the deer pants for streams of water, / so my soul pants for you, O God. / My soul thirsts for God, for the living God." Saint Augustine said that our souls will never find their rest until they find it in God. *He* is the treasure. Our longings will point the way to Him every single time. Each longing in my life that I have discovered, or that has discovered me, drives me to confront a truth that I might not have confronted otherwise: I need God. I am thirsty for God. Desperately thirsty. In every area of my life. I was made by Him and for Him, and apart from Him, I will not be satisfied. My desires for things to fill me and make me whole bear witness to the One who will fill me ultimately. My longing to be known reveals to me the existence of a greater knowing by the One who created me. My hunger for heaven gently sings to me a haunting lullaby that reminds me where we've come from and why we'll never feel fully at home here.

> "The hunger for status is simply a swollen manifestation of the God-given longing for respect."
> —Karen Lee-Thorp and Cynthia Hicks,
> Why Beauty Matters

It is easy to miss this. Listen closely to your longings. I have veered off into sin and missed the treasure on many trips. Sin is trying to meet legitimate needs in an illegitimate way. Every sin that we choose to commit is tied to some very real need in our lives. We try to meet that need or longing with something or someone who cannot meet it. We say to God, "I don't trust You to take care of this situation, or fill this longing, so I will do it myself." We are fooled that the treasure is really the food, or the affair, not the living God.

Recipe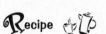

Mocha Fudge Sauce

Great for dipping fruit, topping ice cream, drizzling over any dessert plate, or eating by the spoonful!

3 tablespoons butter
3 ounces unsweetened chocolate
1/2 cup strong coffee, liquid
1/4 cup light corn syrup
1 cup sugar
1 teaspoon vanilla

In a saucepan, melt butter and chocolate. Stir in remaining ingredients except vanilla. Bring sauce to a boil and continue boiling gently, without stirring, until thick and smooth, about 10 minutes. Add vanilla. Serve sauce immediately, or store in the refrigerator.

Sandra

Sandra came to a women's conference to get a closer walk with God. She got a wake-up call to listen to her longings. She asked me if I would pray for her. "I'm having an affair," she confessed. She started crying. "I've been married for nineteen years, and I'm so lonely. My husband was abusive for fifteen years. He got help, and now he doesn't abuse me anymore, but I'm afraid that I don't love him." Now she was sobbing. I just held her. I prayed for wisdom. I hurt with her. "I went back to school two years ago, but my husband doesn't like it. He never asks me about my grades or anything."

"Did you meet the other man at school?"

She nodded. "His name is Jerry."

"Tell me how Jerry makes you feel." Her face softened, tears still rolling down. "Like I matter. Like I'm important." She paused, wiping tears. "He cares about me, and he thinks I'm beautiful, and he wants to marry me."

Now I'm wiping tears. "Sandra, what you want from Jerry is what every woman wants. We all long to be cared for and thought of as beautiful. That's how we were made. And that's not wrong, or bad." She stared at the floor, listening. "We get into trouble when we think that a man is the one who meets that longing." She looked up at me as I continued.

"But I thought . . ." She stopped.

"We all did. Every woman thinks she's going to meet the perfect man, fall in love, get married, and feel loved and cared for, the rest of her life. But it doesn't work that way. Because we were made to want more."

Sandra asked, "More what?"

"More love than any man can give us."

More tears.

"When someone like Jerry walks into your life and turns a light on inside you, it feels wonderful." She smiled. "And you start to think, *Here's someone who can really love me.* And as a woman, you have a choice. You can embrace the person who turned on the light, or you can embrace the light."

"Oh my . . ." She stopped to think. "You mean what I really want is not Jerry?"

"You want Jerry on one level, but Jerry will not ultimately satisfy you." Sandra sat, head bowed, tears dripping in her lap. "You're so disappointed in your marriage because you cannot get what you are longing for."

I held her, and we both wept. After a bit, I asked her, "What do you think you are really longing for?"

She cried the cry of every woman: "I want to be loved and cherished." By listening to her longings, she was drawn to the right arms. "It's God I really want."

God is the only One big enough to hold our longings. He created them, and when we bring them to Him, we have finally found the right place. Emilie Griffin wrote in *Clinging*, "This is the one intimacy of which we need not be afraid, for it will not disappoint or betray us. On God we can loose all the intensity of what we are, all the passion and the longing we feel. This is the one surrender we can make in utter trust, knowing that we can rest our whole weight there and nothing will give way."

F̶resh-Brewed Adventures

- Write a letter to God, confiding in Him your deepest longings.
- Poetry is the language of longings. Write a poem about one particular longing.
- Take one hour this week and go on a date with yourself. Schedule it on your calendar. Bring your journal and your Bible, and go to your favorite coffee shop, sit on your deck, check out a new art store, or get in the bathtub. Wherever you are, the goal is to create a space to be still and listen to your longings.

Learning to Listen

Life is not a paint-by-number. The right formula is not going to solve our longings. Painting red in compartment number 22

Never reheat coffee. It loses its peak flavor after about twenty minutes.

63

64

may be what someone told you to do, but chances are good that your heart is not going to respond when you force it. When Sandra stoped to listen to what she was really longing for, she came to the conviction that it was not Jerry. She now owns that conviction, because it came from her own soul. Longings will not be "fixed." Ever. Sandra will never get to a place where she doesn't want to be loved, and neither will we. Is our Christian faith about trying to kill our desire to be loved or about surrendering our longings to Christ? Longings are wrestled with, surrendered to God, wrestled with again, lived with, agonized over, laughed about, wrestled with again . . . In the wrestling process, here are some things we can do.

Feel. Get your journal out. Write down some of your wishes and dreams, then identify the longings in them. Allow yourself to feel the pain of where your needs and wants are not being met. Is your marriage all that you desire it to be? Are there disappointments in your family? Is your job satisfying? Listen to what your heart is saying as you ask yourself these questions. Let the answers shape you. What dreams have you given up on? Pay attention, in spite of the hurt. Skip the morphine. Cut up the credit cards and leave the chocolate at the store. Let yourself feel the longing. Feeling keeps our hearts tender and our souls open to be directed to God.

Discern. Is there an area of your life that feels out of control right now? Is there an unmet longing driving the behavior? Dig deep until you find it. Be aware that our greatest temptations always come from our longings. Like Sandra, when we are wrestling with the longing to be known, we are in a prime position to be tempted by an affair. Bad spending patterns or cycles of overeating can be broken by uncovering the longing to be filled and taking it to the right place. Don't be afraid to admit your vulnerability. In our denial, we can be blindsided by the force of our cravings. Learning to discern as we listen can keep us from making mistakes with cheap substitutions.

Grieve. "What am I supposed to do?" I asked my counselor one day. "There are places in me that feel so empty. I cannot fill them up. I know sinful things to do, but I don't want to do them. What do I do?" I was close to tears.

65

The burden is too great at times, the struggle too intense for us not to just let go. My counselor looked at me with a knowing that comes from having walked this road, and said, "Put your head on the chest of God and weep." I couldn't have stopped the tears then if I'd tried. I wept, openly, for a long time. *Put your head on the chest of God and weep.* Cry a river. Let it go. The energy that it takes to hold it all together would be better spent on other things, like healing.

When I pulled myself together enough to speak, I said, "I think I'm dying."

He leaned in and responded, "I think you're living." I sat there for a moment. If this was living, I wasn't sure if I wanted life. But then I recognized the gentle voice of my Savior, telling me that He would be with me in the deepest parts of my life. Many times for me counseling is just having a safe place to cry.

> "All my longings lie open before you, O Lord; / my sighing is not hidden from you."
> —Psalm 38:9

In *Heart to Heart About Men*, Nancy Groom wrote, "For most of my life I would not grieve, because it was seen as a weakness: Strong women don't grieve. Now I believe *only* strong women can grieve, and it's a weakness *not* to grieve . . . I don't think Jesus named the Holy Spirit the Comforter just on a whim."

Until we grieve we cannot be comforted. Until we lay our longings at the feet of Jesus we cannot be ministered to by His presence. Until I come to the end of "longings management"—trying to hold it all together, I can't trust Christ. But when I bring Him my crumpled longings, from holding them so tightly in my fist, He will hold them for me. He will be enough.

66

Give. I have a friend, Julie, who has a tremendous longing to have a family. Probably more of a dream than a longing, because it could be a reality one day. She loves kids and teenagers. The problem is, she's not married. With no ship in sight on the horizon, she is simply left with dreaming that gives way at times to raw longing. She's not out looking for a husband.

> "It seems to me we can never give up longing and wishing while we are thoroughly alive."
> —George Eliot (Mary Ann Evans), English writer

She's not desperate in the least, just longing. She has brought that longing to God, laid it at the feet of Jesus, and now she serves others out of that longing. She ministers in her church to teenagers and students. She's not waiting on anything or anybody but God. She opens her home and has kids over all the time. She celebrates the passion in the longing. She embraces her yearning and ministers powerfully out of it. She connects through her longings and allows God to use them to draw people to Himself.

Laugh. Laughter works on the soul like medicine. There are a couple of friends that I love going to lunch with. So much healing comes from laughter. We laugh about men, we laugh about longing for heaven. When we finally get around to looking at a menu, we laugh about our longing to be filled. When the waiter comes to take our order, we can hardly get the words out, as one of us invariably orders, "One of everything, please, with cheese." Our longings, as they are discussed with friends, create a bond that wouldn't come if we simply stayed on the surface. Real laughter and enjoyment come from going deep and then rising to the surface to get air. The laughter is like bubbles on the way up.

Anticipate. Can you recall the feelings of sheer delight

you experienced as a child when you thought about what Christmas would be like if it would ever arrive? Anticipation is the secret gift of longing. The hope is often greater than the realization. The excitement of a vacation and the energy spent dreaming up plans are often better than taking the actual trip. There is something incredibly powerful about waiting. It keeps our hearts ready and open. Waiting and wondering are treasures to us when we are not overly focused on "getting there."

Waiting works this truth into our souls: sometimes not having is better than having. If for no other reason than the way it makes us feel. Emilie Griffin put it this way in *Clinging:* We can learn to do without something when we come to "an understanding that not-tasting is better than tasting . . . It is a comprehension of the falsity of sampling experience as a way to fulfillment . . . an understanding that doing without pleasure, the emptiness that makes itself empty for God . . . is a deeper experience of truth than the constant rush to plunge into and taste things."

Trust. God has not forgotten you. When God says no to a longing, it is because not filling it will shape us more than filling it would. These longings are in our lives to shape us by the wanting. We are becoming more like Christ, often by suffering, by being finely ground.

The happiest women I know are the spiritually mature. They aren't giddy happy, they are free happy. Their marriages are good, but they are not everything they ever longed for. They look to God to meet their ultimate needs. No woman is free from disappointment, but they bring their disappointment to Christ, trusting that He is using it in their lives. That's the kind of trust I want, and the kind of woman I want to be. Finding comfort in the fact that I belong body and soul to my faithful Savior, Jesus Christ.

Hope. God gives us some powerful promises to live by. We are not without hope. He has given us His word that one day we will live in a better place than here. A place where our long-ings will be met. First Corinthians 13, verse 9, reminds us that "for now we only know in part. We love in part, we speak truth in part." Everything is in part. Can you remember when you were children? You loved as children love, simple and free. It was good, but it wasn't even close to what it would be. And remember when you grew older? You loved as an adult, pas-sionate and committed. But one day—one glorious day—we will love as God loves. Right now, it's like looking in one of those mirrors that isn't glass. It's really difficult to see anything. You get an image, but there's no definition. However, one day we will see Him face-to-face—His glorious face to our less-than-we-want-it-to-be face. Right now we can only see a dim reflection, but one day we will look into His eyes—the eyes that have seen from the foundation of the world. "Now I know in part . . . then I shall know fully, even as I am fully known."

All of our hungers, all of our longings will melt in the power of His gaze when it meets ours. Everything we were created to be will be evident, and we will know as we are known. We will *feel* known by God. I can hardly imagine it. We will be whole, filled, and satisfied. All of our pain, every last ounce of our sor-row, any emptiness that we have felt will vanish like the morn-ing dew. Gone. We will kneel in His presence in a place where there are no tears and where lions lie down with lambs. The intensity of His love and the encompassing of His embrace will overwhelm us. As our hearts finally receive all that we have longed for, I imagine some will dance, some will weep, but all of us will know we are home, at last.

EMBRACE YOUR BEAUTY

The terror creeps up my spine before I even get out of bed. I know what lies ahead today. I stay completely still and let the safety of the covers envelop me. Maybe if I ignore it, it will go away. The hard work that will fill my day already drains every ounce of energy in my body. The dread of all the walking, the endless barrage of searching, the tears.

I have to buy a swimsuit today.

What is it about that one purchase that makes my knees weak and my self-esteem plummet? Maybe it's thinking about looking at my body under lights that pick up things the Hubble telescope would miss. Maybe it's the fact that the top of my legs look like the surface of the moon. Perhaps it's the futility of trying to make a stretchy piece of fabric the size of a pot holder cover the square mile of my rear end. But somehow this one activity moves me from a self-confident, mature woman to feeling like I'm back in junior high.

You finally get to the point where you just don't care. You learn to get over it and give up things. Let it go. It just doesn't matter: I don't ever have to swim again.

70

I remember a TV commercial with Cybill Shepherd lounging on a sofa, running her fingers through her hair, saying, "Don't hate me because I'm beautiful." I was ten and didn't hate Cybill. I thought she was beautiful, and I was sad that she thought women would hate her for that. Now I'm thirty-two, and guess what? I hate her. I've had twenty-two years to grow tired of the obsession with beauty in our culture. I cannot escape it. Commercials, magazine ads, movies, infomercials, books—everywhere a woman turns in this world, someone shoves an airbrushed beauty in our faces trying to sell us something. It used to be just products; now it's self-esteem, or a better life. As if a beautiful face or the perfect body means a better life. But you begin to wonder.

We are literally pulled in two by our feelings about beauty. We "know" all the right answers about this. We "know" that beauty is on the inside, and we shouldn't pursue it too passionately, but what woman doesn't want to be beautiful? And the church doesn't help, by telling us it's not "spiritual" to spend too much time looking in the mirror. This just makes us *pretend* that we don't. "This old thing?" We hear a minister with a frowning face say, "You don't think Mother Teresa worried about beauty, do you?" There is some truth in that, but while I want to love like Mother Teresa, I don't want to look like Mother Teresa. We're guilted into rejecting our desire to be beautiful, but we can't reject it completely. So we stay in no-man's-land, the zone, on the fence, between the lines, pulled in two directions.

Female Schizophrenia

I think *Vogue* is a magazine for skinny women who wear clothes that are too small. But I still buy it.

I think the fashion industry is outlandish, and I wouldn't

be caught dead wearing some of that stuff, even to a Halloween party. But I still try it on.

I think face-lifts and cosmetic surgery can be destructive. It makes me mad that women feel the pressure to go to such lengths to hold on to "beauty." But I've thought about it.

I rant and rave over the *Sports Illustrated* swimsuit issue. I am angry over the exploitation of women and the way men are so drawn to their bodies. But I wish I had a body like that.

We pretend we don't care. But we do.

We act as if it doesn't matter. But it does.

We wish we weren't disappointed. But we are.

Why Embrace Beauty?

For some women, beauty has been the enemy. Beauty, or the perceived lack of it, has been the cause of painful rejections, missed promotions, struggles in marriage, or even self-hatred. Given the challenge, let alone the opportunity, to embrace beauty seems about as dumb as trying to spit into the wind. We're scared. Isn't it better, we reason, to dismiss beauty than to try to embrace something that we fear we don't have? Won't we look foolish if we think we are beautiful when we are not? All of these were my thoughts as I began to think about how negative I had become toward beauty. I was so afraid that I didn't have "it" that I rejected it before "it" or anyone could reject me.

What I miss in this thinking is what not embracing beauty does to me and to my spirit. The more I dismiss beauty as belonging to others, the more I reject opportunities to nurture my spirit, the more I hold my physical appearance at arm's length and try not to care, the more I die on the inside.

Karen Lee-Thorp and Cynthia Hicks wrote in *Why Beauty Matters*, "Our bodies are as much us as our thoughts are. This

72

is why calls to ignore our outer appearance as spiritually irrelevant do not help us. Quite the contrary: the more we honor our bodies as us, as intertwined with our spirits, as limbs of Christ, temples of the Spirit, and bearers of God's image, the more we will understand and manage well the power of physical appearance in our lives."

We must embrace our beauty because beauty is a part of who God created us to be. We are mind, body, and soul. Each of these elements possesses beauty in its own right and deserves to be embraced. That embracing transforms us to live our lives in a whole and healthy, honoring-to-God way. Are we seeking to embrace beauty so that the world will accept us? No. Beauty needs to be redeemed unto the Lord. Do we embrace beauty so we can look as if we have it all together spiritually? No. Beauty is embraced because we don't have it all together, and we are trusting God in a more radical way than ever before to make something beautiful out of our surrendered lives.

Embracing our beauty will wake us up. We'll have to face all the parts that we have deemed ugly and worthless. We'll be confronted by old pains and wounds, and we'll have to make a choice to stay dead or to give way to new growth and life. We'll be challenged by what not embracing our beauty does to our families and our relationships. Consider the possibilities: you can learn to embrace your beauty and allow it to bring you joy and delight, or you can give in to the culture's definition of beauty and allow that to rob you of every shred of confidence and enthusiasm you have about who you are.

Linda

She never looks in the mirror. She showers quickly and wraps the towel around her tightly. She dresses in her closet, even away from her husband. She buys clothes that are a little

Coffee was first known in Europe as Arabian wine.

too big for fear that something will cling and reveal her ugly shape. She privately criticizes other women for dressing inappropriately. She prides herself on her modesty. *So I'm heavier than I want to be,* she thinks to herself, *At least I'm not parading my body around.* She watches her husband constantly to be certain he is not looking at other women. She listens intently during sermons about beauty, priding herself that she doesn't struggle with vanity like other women. *There is one advantage to being ugly: at least I'm not proud.* During infrequent sex, Linda wants the lights off and the covers on.

Fresh-Brewed Adventures

- Write a letter to your mother about her beauty.
- If you've never spent a day at a spa, go for it. Get a massage and a facial, maybe a manicure or a pedicure. Treat yourself to a kindness day.
- If you've done the spa day before, try a listening retreat, for your soul. Find a spiritual director, and spend half a day with God.

Jill

She exercises regularly and wears clothes that fit her form. Jill isn't completely satisfied with her body, but she enjoys her shape and feels attractive. She takes baths and isn't afraid to look at her body in the mirror and survey its contour. She takes time to get ready and usually feels confident about her appearance in public. She spends a fair amount of money on clothes because she recognizes that they are important for the expression as well as the perception of who she is. She sees her husband's eye caught by a beautiful woman, and laughs. "What do you think is beautiful about her?" she asks, really wanting to know. She doesn't feel threatened, she feels secure in who she is. Jill wants the covers off and the lights on, a lot.

There is nothing spiritual about hating your own body. So much of what we call humility, and even modesty, is merely veiled loathing of the way we were made. Other words for vanity are airs, arrogance, condescension, disdain. Of the two women described above, Linda is far more vain and obsessed about her appearance. It is an indirect vanity, invisible from the outside, that holds her hostage. It's a complete failure to trust God. Jill lives a fresh-brewed life. She knows how to embrace her beauty.

> "The mass media often trivialize our lives and our achievements, narrowing the litmus test of female worth to one question: Does she have dimpled thighs or crow's feet? If so, onto the trash heap of history."
> —Susan Douglas

I know these women well. They are both me. I was "Linda" for the first five years of our marriage. Beginning counseling, waking up to my life, embracing the Lover of my soul, has changed my life. If anyone had tried to tell Linda that one day she would be Jill, I would have laughed in her face. I still have Linda days, but I confess, I love being Jill. Actually, I love being Nicole.

Obstacles to Embracing Your Beauty

By placing so much emphasis on beauty, while trying not to at the same time, we put ourselves at odds with beauty constantly. We don't gently embrace it, we try to seize it. It eludes us, and we reject it. It comes back to us, and we dismiss it like a lover spurned. We have a bittersweet relationship with beauty. We can't embrace beauty at all until we recognize the obstacles that keep us from trusting it.

We don't like ourselves. Let's face it, most of us don't like the way we look. Sad, but true. We constantly criticize our appearance and berate our bodies. We don't receive compliments well because we don't believe them.

Consider these statistics, quoted in *Why Beauty Matters:* "A 1995 study found that 48 percent of American women felt 'wholesale displeasure' about their bodies. That is, about half of us utterly detest our appearance, while many more merely dislike our weight or breasts or thighs. This self-hatred has spiraled up from 23 percent in 1972 and 38 percent in 1985."

We aren't getting better, we are getting worse.

The emphasis on beauty in our culture has women rejecting themselves in epidemic proportions. We think that if we could eliminate the problems that we see in our bodies then we could accept ourselves. We are drawn into a downward spiral of eating disorders and self-rejecting behaviors that leave us with complete disdain for who we are.

We compare constantly. Most of us could say, "I feel really good about myself until I turn on the television, or look at a magazine, or watch a movie, or stand in the checkout line at the grocery, or look at the Victoria's Secret catalog, or meet anyone thinner than I am. If I don't do any of those things, I'm fine!"

All women are assaulted on an hourly basis by an invisible attacker: comparison. We have spent years deciding if we're pretty based on how we measure up to all the images swirling around us. But we measure ourselves not only against media stereotypes, but against every other woman we know. Do you walk into a room and find yourself scanning it for anyone who might be more attractive than you? Women watch other women more than men do! We are weighing ourselves against other women. *Am I thinner than she is? Do I look like that in my swimsuit? Her hair is beautiful; I wonder if mine will do that?* How terribly sad to have so little confidence in our own worth as women that we can only find value in relation to others.

76

Nothing good ever comes from comparing ourselves to other women. When we compare ourselves and feel that we come out favorably, we become haughty. When we compare and don't measure up, we become ungrateful for what we do have. Comparison never leads to humility or compassion or acceptance. To become arrogant or ungrateful will send us toward self-rejection faster than you can say L'Oreal.

We listen to voices from the past. What events in your past shaped the way that you feel about yourself and how you look? Who had the most impact positively or negatively on your sense of beauty? Get out your journal and start to jot things down as they occur to you.

When I was ten years old, the unthinkable happened: I began to grow breasts. What an inconvenience. Breasts were not useful to me at ten, nor were they desirable. They didn't aid in climbing trees or sliding into second, and as far as I was concerned, they were over-rated (I still feel that way, a little). Well, my mother decided it was time to shop for a bra. Could there be anything more humiliating than missing your playtime after school to go to Sears with your mom to try on an uncomfortable harness that you didn't ever want to wear anyway? When my mother informed my stepfather of our journey, he piped up, "She doesn't need a bra, she needs Band-Aids!"

> "The most beautiful make-up of a woman is passion. But cosmetics are easier to buy."
> —Yves St. Laurent

I was mortified.

I may not have wanted these growths on my chest, but I wanted to be made fun of even less. Band-Aids! Now I had to be concerned with the fact that I might not be normal. Maybe

I would never fully "develop," as they called it back then. Like a photograph that you don't have to pay for when you pick up your pictures at Wal-Mart. I would be "underdeveloped." That's major at ten years old. Funny, yes. Painful, you bet. I still remember it. The message I heard was that my breasts were small, and small breasts deserve to be made fun of. It is a message that I have carried with me all my life. In fact the other day I made a comment to a friend: "One great thing about having small breasts is that nobody wonders if they're real!" I have learned to laugh, but that laughter was born of pain, and it still affects how I feel about myself.

We are held hostage by pain. In *The Face of Love*, Ellen Lambert reveals an event in her childhood, her mother's death, that radically altered her view on beauty:

> I understand now that the transformation of myself from a beautiful child to an ugly one is so distressing to me because deep down I have known all along what it was: a response to an overwhelming loss. When I look at those early photos of myself I realize that what I am seeing and responding to so positively is the way delight and security inform a child's whole physical aspect. Looking at the photographs closely, I realize how many of the details I read as "beauty" can be referred back to the love at the center of that charmed circle . . . all those outward-reaching, confident gestures, of a body at peace with itself in the world. And so it comes to me now, with the same rush of understanding, that what I am responding to, when I look at the images of myself sitting awkwardly on someone else's porch, with the wrong dress and the wrong hairstyle, and features which seem to have lost their right relation to one another, is the enormity of the loss that wrought such a change . . . I didn't just *become* ugly; my ugliness in

those later childhood years was a response—in a sense *the most powerful response* I could make—to the turning upside down of my whole life.

I was on a plane when I read her story. I had to close the book and cry. When my parents divorced and my life was turned upside down, I felt the deepest awareness of loss I had ever known. But I had no words for it. My body, posture, hair, and disposition responded for me. Very little was "right" in my life after that. I, too, have pictures of looking completely out of place, wearing the wrong thing, in some "other family's" home. On the plane I opened my journal and wrote, *Pain always finds a way out. Like water seeking low ground, pain worked its way through my body, affecting everything about the way I looked until it found its way out.* Beautiful children are the ones who know they are loved and accepted. A bright smile, confidence, and warmth are born in the soul of one who feels loved. Without love and acceptance, any hope of beauty goes with it.

> "Genius is of small use to a woman who does not know how to do her hair."
> —Edith Wharton

Karen Lee-Thorp spoke for all of us when she wrote, "I didn't need people to tell me what colors I looked best in so much as I needed people who gave me reasons to wear happy colors instead of sad ones."

We put our beauty in the hands of men. Did you date guys who respected you, or did you have to "prove" yourself and your worth just to keep the relationship? It's amazing what one or two early, bad relationships can do to our self-concept. "You should cut your hair in feathers like Farrah Fawcett's." Thank you. "You should wear more dresses, not jeans so much like guys do." Okay. "Why don't you smile more? You're too serious." I tried too hard to be everything that any guy wanted me to be. I felt horrible about myself, and dating was not helping. I was so hungry for love and acceptance that my self-worth was a small price to pay for any tidbit. So when a relationship ended, I took that to a very personal place inside of me. I spray-painted "defective" on the wall of my soul.

Then I met Paul. As in every relationship before him, I handed over the keys of my beauty to him, and he dropped them. Except this time I was married and I couldn't leave. Paul didn't intend to let me down. And he didn't "drop the keys" because he's a bad person, or even because he's a man—any person to whom we try to hand the keys of our beauty will drop them, because they are human and flawed. This is true of our own expectations and demands as well. But I had rested my entire self-concept on how Paul felt about me. So when that foundation crumbled, it brought me to this awareness: we will never embrace our real beauty if we are only trying to please someone else.

Many women live with men who hold impossible standards of what they feel their wife should look like. That is devastating to a relationship. Karen Lee-Thorpe wrote, "To the degree that a woman lives (or believes she lives) with a man or a culture of men who worship beauty, to that degree she will feel pressure to worship beauty as well." Sadly true. We cannot change our husbands or boyfriends, but we can try to get untangled from their standards. We can seek to embrace our beauty for ourselves rather than merely to please them. It would also be easy to react to their standards in a negative way and treat ourselves poorly to spite them. We both lose in the process.

A Powerful Force

Beauty is heady stuff. Women know this. We know that while a woman may not want beauty to have a substantial role in her life, she'd be foolish not to notice the role it plays in the world.

80

Beauty means control. Cynthia Hicks, in *Why Beauty Matters*, confessed, "To me, weight (not grades or hours spent in prayer) was the ultimate symbol of a woman in control of her life. Fat was the ultimate symbol of weakness and failure. I did not come up with these ideas on my own; I picked them up from the people around me."

How a woman looks instantly identifies her either as someone who has her act together or someone who can't cut the mustard. Today it isn't enough to be smart, hardworking, talented, or anything else if you aren't in shape as well. To be able to pull off a corporate merger or handle the five o'clock feeding frenzy at your home is of little worth if you don't have buns of steel. A woman who works hard all day long but doesn't wear a size six can still be thought of as lazy.

Susan Douglas wrote in *Where the Girls Are*, "Perfect thighs, in other words, were an achievement, a product, and one to be admired and envied. They demonstrated that the woman had made something of herself, that she was the master of her body and, thus, of her fate. If she had conquered her own adipose tissue, she could conquer anything."

Beauty means money. The culture credits thin, beautiful people as being the smart ones in control of their lives. They demonstrate this belief by a bigger paycheck. How you look directly affects what you get paid and how you are treated. Consider these statistics from *Why Beauty Matters:* "Studies in 1986 and 1989 found that with each additional attractiveness point on the researcher's scale, a woman gained $2,000 in ongoing yearly salary. By 1993, people perceived as good-looking—men and women—were earning at least 5 percent more than those labeled average-looking."

Beauty means respect. A woman who is beautiful is perceived as having something to say. When a man stands up to speak, people listen and decide whether they like him based on his content, and then they notice that he doesn't look half bad. Conversely, when a woman stands up to speak, they evaluate her appearance and then decide if they care what she has to say. But be careful. If you are too beautiful, women think you don't have anything to say because you've obviously spent too much time on your appearance.

It's a trap.

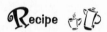

Recipe

Low-Fat Coffee Shake

1 cup skim milk

1 1/2 teaspoons sugar

1 tablespoon instant coffee

1 1/2 tablespoons nonfat powdered milk

Put all ingredients in a blender, cover, and blend until smooth and foamy. Serve in a tall glass over ice.

Like Mother Like Daughter

When your twelve-year-old, ninety-pound daughter starts obsessing about her weight or wanting to go on a diet, something is wrong. It may not be completely the world's fault. Yes, girls do go to school, and they are bombarded by the same media that we are, but do we model love and acceptance ourselves? If we reject ourselves or our beauty, we'd better get ready to see our daughters do the same.

A woman named Julia told her story in *Why Beauty Matters:*

There are over three trillion coffee trees worldwide.

82

When I was very young, I thought that my mother was beautiful . . . Then one day, I saw her look in the mirror and grimace at her reflection. I was confused. I asked her what was the matter and she said she looked "ghastly" without her makeup. I also remember her complaining that she had nothing to wear even though I thought her wardrobe was vast and magical. By the time I was six or seven, I realized that my beautiful mother did not think she was beautiful at all. That made me sad—and it made me sad to see her not eating in order to get thinner. I remember wondering why someone as beautiful as my mother would think she was ugly. And then why did she tell me I was so pretty? What did it mean to be pretty? Was I pretty enough to look in the mirror and like what I see?

Our daughters need to see us embrace our beauty. You are their mother, you are not being evaluated on your stylishness or figure. It is so important not to criticize yourself in front of your daughter or dismiss her compliments. When you model self-hatred, your little girl will model it too. When you diet, she will want to be thinner, because you show her that you value thin-

"If thigh reducing creams really work, why don't they make your hand smaller?"
—Rita Rudner, comedian

ness. That isn't all bad, when it leads to eating well and exercising—just be careful.

I, too, thought my mother was the prettiest mother in the world. I loved watching her put on makeup or curl her hair. I remember sitting on the floor just staring up at my beautiful mother. But she could not appreciate her own beauty. She deflected my compliments. Over the years it completely discounted my ability to believe her when she told me I was beautiful. I learned how to deflect compliments too. I thought she was a poor judge of beauty because she couldn't recognize her own.

Directed Journaling

- Make two columns on your journal page. Write the names of your family members who communicated to you that you had worth and value. Underneath their names write some of the things they said that stand out in your mind. Was there anyone who told you that you were beautiful? Any special aunts or uncles or grandparents? Write their words in your journal.
- Now think through some of the negative messages you received. Who in your family caused you to question your worth? Was there a sibling or parent who constantly criticized your appearance? Was your father able to express his love to you? Write out prayers of forgiveness.
- For most of us, the second side of the page will be a lot easier to fill in. Not only do we remember the negative far more than we do the positive, but chances are good that there wasn't as much positive.

Four Ways to Embrace Your Beauty

Uncovering the things that went wrong in shaping our concept of beauty is helpful to the degree that it enables us to move on to the present. There is no way to embrace beauty in our lives when we can't live in the present. When we are plagued by doubts from the past or when fear of aging drives us to fret over the future, we aren't free to embrace our beauty.

1. Be Kind to Yourself

SARK, my favorite creative writer, noticed, "Women are very good at shining kindness outward, yet if you ask them how kind they are to themselves, they often cry." I don't know why we treat ourselves so poorly, but we do. We think it's more spiritual. We say mean things when we disappoint ourselves: *If you were a better Christian, you wouldn't have done that!* We say things to ourselves that we would never say to others: *When are you going to lose some weight? You are so fat! Look at yourself!*

If you are unhappy with your weight, or any area of your life, don't beat yourself up. It solves nothing. Shaming yourself for whatever reason will not take the pounds off. In my life, shame starts me on a cycle of putting more pounds on. "I haven't reduced my thighs or my butt. I haven't given up potato chips. I haven't read my Bible three days in a row." And I won't do any of that when I treat myself that way. It used to work for me, but it doesn't anymore. Whipping myself into shape used to produce some results, but now it only makes me tired and sore. How do you take care of yourself? Try kindness. Try accepting where you are. Try forgiving yourself for not being all you want to be. Try nurturing your soul when you want to despise it.

Let's try to help each other in this. I appreciate the advice SARK gave us: "When you see your 'sister' beating up on herself, take her weapons away and just hold her."

2. Listen to the Longing

I found out there is another Nicole Johnson. I discovered this when she won the Miss America Pageant. All I need in my life to compound this beauty dilemma is to be confused with the most beautiful woman alive. No pressure. It's not a problem in person—no confusion there. But on the radio or in print, we are both open for mistakes in identity. In fact, if you bought this book thinking I was Miss America, I hope I haven't disappointed you. If I have, welcome to the cold, hard reality of being a woman. Only one in a gazillion women is ever going to be Miss America. I never really thought it would be me. I never was disappointed that I wasn't Miss America. I never even thought about it much. Until this year when I realized I would never be Miss America. It was too late for me, and time had passed for the opportunity, not to mention the qualifications. A sadness settled on me. I had to grieve.

85

Wanting to be beautiful is a longing. We can't reject the longing to be lovely. We should listen to it and discern what it is saying to us. We cannot be dominated by it or try to meet it in inappropriate ways, but we must acknowledge that

> "'I am beautiful to the one who loves me.' or 'I will be loved if I am beautiful.' In the gap between those two statements, thousands of women live in fear and sorrow."
> —Karen Lee-Thorp and Cynthia Hicks
> Why Beauty Matters

it exists and that we are drawn to it. Like every longing, it is telling us something. We were made for more. We are daughters of Eve. We were created in God's image, and we are beautiful. But we are fallen, and we live in a fallen world that cannot value beauty as God has created it. Therefore, we are left longing.

But in the midst of my longing, I received this e-mail from a friend:

Is this Nicole Johnson's e-mail? Is this *the* Nicole Johnson? The best selling author, the popular speaker, the long driver, the sweet singer, the marathon runner, the interior decorator, the stay up late get up early never met a challenge she didn't like Nicole Johnson? Is this the stay the course, dwell in the word, raise your hands and sing Nicole Johnson? Is this the e-mail literate,

hi-tech hi-touch 90's soon to be 00's leader Nicole
Johnson?
—or is this just Miss America?

This e-mail reminds me to be grateful to God for who He
created *me* to be. And grateful for the gift of a friend who sees
more in me than I often see in myself.

3. Discover the Secret

There is no beauty in makeup. Expensive clothes will not
make you beautiful. The secret lies in being an alive, awake
woman with something to offer the world. Namely, yourself.
Beauty is less about your face and more about your smile. Less
about the shape of your eyebrows, more about the light in your
eyes. Less about the length of your legs, more about the
bounce in your step. Real beauty is being a viable, vital human
being. As you participate in your life with a warm smile and a
generous spirit, you are beautiful.

All my life I thought beauty was what I looked like. Now I
understand it's so much more than that. Beauty cannot be separated into its component parts. It is a package of things that
reveal someone's beauty, not one thing. Someone may have
thick, shiny hair, but having lovely hair doesn't necessarily
make one beautiful.

Living a fresh-brewed life will bring out the beauty in you
because it is uncovering you. It is revealing more of the authentic you that is beautiful. Fresh-brewed life helps us find the reason to wear happy colors, or sets us free to wear black, without
it being a statement. Color becomes very important to us.
Because life is a living, breathing work of art. We are painting
as we go. What shades reveal most clearly who you are? Never
forget you have magnificent hues at your disposal. Discover
them, and finger paint all over your life! Be a masterpiece.
Drink in life. Laugh too loud. Compliment others constantly.

Coffee is the second highest consumed beverage after water.

Cultivate beauty all around you. Plant a garden. Embrace beauty wherever you find it—in the fall leaves, in the spring flowers. This will help you embrace it in yourself. When you appreciate a sunset or your child's clay candlestick or a beautiful piece of music, you are saying yes to beauty. You are saying yes to God.

4. Embrace the Lover of Your Soul

It is so easy to believe that God is silent on the subject of beauty. Maybe it is because the church is silent, or maybe it's because we have to be so still to hear what God is saying. Either way, so many women simply think God is not saying anything about how they feel about themselves. Here is the simple, fresh-brewed truth: God is loving us passionately and intensely, and that love has nothing to do with the way we look. It isn't affected one ounce by the size of our blue jeans or the way our nose slopes up or how much dental work we've had done. It isn't lessened by wearing the wrong dress to a party or having no skill in applying makeup or by hating exercise. God simply loves us as we are. Which also means that if we get in shape or find a great hairstyle or learn to wear colors that look great on us, God still loves us. But He doesn't love us any more. We haven't "gone up in His eyes" or improved in His estimation of us. He loves us. Right now. Exactly where we are.

But before we just gloss over that and go right on to the next thing, let me ask a hard question. Have you let that truth into your soul? I mean, really let it in? God is the One who has never criticized you or belittled you or made fun of your appearance in any way. He is the One who formed you, and said afterward, "This is good."

In Luke, chapter 7, "a woman who had lived a sinful life" brought an alabaster jar and broke it at the feet of Jesus. I am certain it was the most beautiful thing she owned. It represented

88

her very life. At His feet, she poured out all her longings, all her struggles, all her attempts to measure up, all her manipulations to try to get love. She poured it all out at the feet of the One who could love her completely. She finally found the right feet. And Jesus was moved. The Pharisees were embarrassed by how honest she had been with Jesus (they always will be, by the way) and wanted Him to send her away. But He would not. He recognized in her a heart of longing. He knew the sinful attempts that she had made to meet them apart from God. He forgave her.

And He will forgive us. We, too, have brought the alabaster jar of who we are to the wrong feet. We have tried to get love from others by using beauty. We have brought our pain to people who could not ease it, though we hoped they could. There is only one set of feet that can heal us. The ones with the holes.

Percolations

Books

Why Beauty Matters, Karen Lee-Thorp and Cynthia Hicks*

The Good Life, Ruth McGinnis

Movies

Babette's Feast

My Fair Lady

Beauty and the Beast

Music

Storms, Nancy Griffith

Carry Us Through, Sarah Masen

Where are you right now? Can you determine in what direction you need to move? If you spend a lot of time focusing on the externals of beauty, ease up and trust more of your inner qualities to take the lead. Work on your spirit and the invisible things that people don't notice immediately.

If you have given up on your outward appearance out of fear or self-rejection, now is a great time to begin healing. A special fragrance or a new pair of shoes can show your soul an act of kindness. Clothes don't define you; they reveal you. Makeup isn't meant to cover anything up; it is intended to help you look as alive as you feel. Start allowing the living, breathing, feeling you to encounter the world in an authentic way, with no apologies!

We apologize too much. SARK wrote, "Stop apologizing and saying, 'I'm sorry' so much. Women have a terrible habit of apologizing for everything (even their own existence). *Sorry* in the dictionary says this: wretched, miserable, inferior in worth or quality. We are NOT this!"

There is freedom from the tyranny of beauty. I am embracing it. If you could see me, you would laugh out loud. I'm sitting at my computer with wet hair in two-day-old clothes. Not a pretty sight. But we live by faith, not by sight. I feel beautiful. Right now. Because I am alive and awake and participating in my life. I am loved and cherished, and I love and cherish others. I am embracing my beauty as I am. Not when I get all the cellulite off my thighs or when my skin is clear or when my breasts increase two sizes. All I have is what God has given me, and I am choosing to accept it. I still feel the longing, but I am grateful for what God has given to me.

For years my mother told me I was beautiful, but I didn't believe her. She told me that beauty wasn't about what I looked like. Today I am at the best place of my life to choose to believe her. And paint my toenails.

P.S. Cybill, I don't hate you.

---

*Karen Lee-Thorp, together with Cynthia Hicks, has written what I believe is the best book on beauty I have ever read. And I have read many. I have been waiting a long time for a book that offers real dialogue and hope on the subject of beauty. I've grown weary of cliché books filled with beauty tips that never touch the heart, or other books that try to disconnect us from our bodies, giving us the mistaken impression that "the outside doesn't matter." It does matter, and in their book *Why Beauty Matters*, they explore that deeply and provide real and honest answers.

INTERVIEW YOUR ANGER

Part One

I slammed the front door, and I got in the car and drove away. Paul and I had just had one of the biggest fights of our marriage. I didn't go far, maybe two blocks. I was already crying, and I was inconsolable. I pulled over on the side of the road and sobbed. I was so angry with him.

It had started with something small. I don't even remember now what he did, but it set me off. We began to argue and fight about "the issue," probably something like not taking the trash out when I asked him to. Whatever it was, I went off. I said some very harsh things to Paul, and "punished him" with my anger. Then he said it. He had no idea his words would change my life and our marriage. "You're just like your mother!" he spat. I felt it like a physical blow.

I couldn't speak. I had no air. I had no comeback. And I had no thoughts of staying in the house any longer. I left Paul standing in the bedroom, dazed. I got my keys, and I slammed the door. I drove two blocks from the house and pulled over. I gripped the steering wheel tighter and tighter until my fingernails cut into my hands. The pain felt good. I wanted to hurt myself.

Paul knew his words would wound me. He knew the history of my relationship with my mother. He was there at our college graduation when she locked herself in my bedroom and would not come out for eight hours. He held me as I wept when Mother decided not to attend our wedding because we wouldn't have a receiving line. He knew that there was nothing I wanted any more in life than to not be like my mother. How could he say that to me? Surely it wasn't true. He was just trying to hurt me. I had made him mad about the trash, and this was his retaliation. So why did I feel undone, exposed, and enraged?

I couldn't stop crying. I yelled at the top of my lungs inside the closed car. The sound hurt my ears. "Why did you say that to me? Why?" I sobbed. "It's not true!" I slammed things around in the car. I couldn't be like my mother. If I had become my mother, my life was over.

Paul's words had come as a complete surprise. At the time, my mother and I weren't speaking and that was very fine by me. I thought by not communicating with her that I had loosened the frightful hold she'd had on my life. I gripped the steering wheel tighter. Why did he say that to me? He had played those words like a trump card and forced my hand.

I was so tempted to keep driving. I didn't want to go home. If I really was like my mother, who was on her fourth marriage, then Paul would get exactly what was coming to him if I left. He didn't love me anyway, I reasoned. How could he if I was like her? I didn't really believe that, though. I knew he did love me, and that made it worse. I knew that to drive on from here and not ever go home again would reveal he was right. And it would kill any hope I had of ever changing. Either way I was stuck. I had lost.

I dragged in the front door of my house, defeated. I crumpled to the floor still crying. Paul came into the kitchen, took one look at me, and put his arms around me. He held me as I wept. I choked out the words, "I want to change." Then Paul said two more words that gave me incredible hope that he still believed in me, and in us—"I know."

Facing the Woman in the Mirror

Coming home was the first step of a lifelong journey to work on my anger. I made a decision that day to look in the mirror, and the face looking back at me was angry.

Anger is so hard for women to admit. We are afraid of it. We don't want to be labeled angry. There is an ugly stigma attached to women who are angry. Men are considered powerful when they are angry. They are leaders, who are forceful or strong. But women who are angry are often labeled shrews, nags, or men-haters, who are irrational or out of control. We get called the ever-popular "B" word. So, we get angry silently. We try to hide our anger. We take our hurt and frustration and bury it like a dog does a bone. We have holes and tunnels beneath every room in our houses. When our husband or friends sense some buried anger beneath the surface, they ask, "What's wrong?"

"Nothing!" we snarl, as we slam things around. But anger is never buried dead, says Gary Smalley. It's always buried alive. It has a way of digging out, especially when we don't want it to. We would rather be anything than "mad." When Paul asks me,

> "Anger repressed can poison a relationship surely as the cruelest words."
>
> —Dr. Joyce Brothers

"Are you mad?" I always lie. Every time. I don't want to be mad, and if I am mad, I certainly don't want him labeling me

94

that way. So I stuff, bury, hide, avoid, deny, close up, and shut down (or think I do). And then, lo and behold, I find myself standing in front of my dryer in a rage or completely reduced to tears because I can't find the mate of my black sock! Or I blow up in the grocery store saying horrible things to the clerk because there is no more Starbucks Ice Cream. Then I have to ask myself, *Where is this coming from? Is it really about socks or ice cream?*

No. Real "ice-cream disappointment" is brief. "Sock anxiety" (even during PMS) is *not* filled with rage. When we find ourselves intensely angry over the little things, or things that should be little things, it's time to wake up. Anger is a signal to heed carefully. When the CHECK ENGINE SOON light comes on in your automobile, there's something you need to pay attention to. Tears in the grocery store are telling you something. Yelling at your children over Legos means your soul is sending you a message: CHECK ENGINE SOON.

But what do you check? Like a good mechanic, your job is to look under the hood and do some investigating to find out what is causing your light to come on. But many women treat their souls the same way they treat their cars. They don't care what's going on under the hood, as long as the car is still running. We think problems will simply "right themselves." I did. I thought that my anger would simply go away. Right. Then Tattoo would come out and welcome me to "Fantasy Island."

Harriet Goldhor Lerner, in her amazing book *The Dance of Anger*, wrote, "Anger is neither legitimate nor illegitimate, meaningful nor pointless. Anger simply is. To ask, 'Is my anger legitimate?' is similar to asking, 'Do I have a right to be thirsty?'"

By holding internal debates over whether or not we should be angry, we hold to an illusion that we are wrestling with our anger or solving it while actually we are doing nothing. Most women want to get the anger out of their lives, but they just

A "Banana Gorilla" is a mocha latte with banana syrup.

don't do anything about it. They talk about it some, but they never change their patterns of relating or do the "work under the hood" to find out what is wrong.

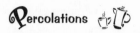

Books

> *The Dance of Anger*, Harriet Goldhor Lerner
> *Making Love Last Forever*, Gary Smalley

Movies

> *When a Man Loves a Woman*
> *Dead Man Walking*
> *The Joy Luck Club*
> *Prince of Tides*

Music

> *Lord of the Past: A Compilation*, Bob Bennett
> *End of Innocence*, Don Henley
> *Steady On*, Shawn Colvin

Surveying the Situation

I propose an interview. This is exactly what is called for in order to take care of ourselves. When your son or daughter comes running into the room, crying that "I'm-in-pain" cry, you immediately look for blood. When you don't see any, you start the interview. "Where does it hurt? What happened? Can you put weight on it?" The answers to the questions are so important because they tell you what your next move is.

The interview is critical because anger is tricky. An immediate or secondary issue might be causing your surface anger, but when you have a major blowup or rage, there is something else bringing fuel to the fire. You have to be a tough interviewer. It might even take a counselor or a friend to interview you. Someone has to be able to ask the hard questions, like, "If you are sitting in your car entertaining thoughts of leaving your husband, knuckles white, crying out of control over the trash not going out, can you see that something is terribly wrong?" My counselor, Ken, helped me see that. He also searched with me to find the leak that led to the underground gas reservoir in my life that fueled much of my anger.

Part Two

My mother left my father when I was five years old. She got my sister and me dressed one summer morning, braided our hair, and packed us and my brother into the convertible for the long drive to Louisiana. We were going to visit MaMa and PaPa. We never went home again. My short, five-year-old life in Florida was completely erased. No more house, no more friends, no more father. We lived in a two-bedroom apartment in Louisiana when I started second grade. Mother was working to support three children. I was the youngest, but no less confused than my older brother and sister. My father would make the seven-hour drive as often as he could, and we would have joyful reunions and agonizing goodbyes. There is no way to explain divorce to a child. It is pure, undiluted pain.

I can picture in my mind the day the battle between them began. We were sitting on a park bench when Dad asked us if we wanted to come and live with him. I thought saying yes was the way to bring our family back together and curb this raw longing for my father. That longing wreaked havoc in my world as our case went to court. Mother and Dad were vying for our loyalty. They were the ones divorcing, and we were the ones on trial.

"Who do you want to live with, Nicole?" I was seated high up, the question came from an attorney below me. From my place on the witness stand, I heard words coming out of my throat, but it was not my voice. I had lost my voice. I had been prepped for weeks, and I knew what I was going to say, but it was not my voice. My voice would have sounded like one long, woeful wail. I simply said, "My mother."

Mother and Dad were bitter enemies. I would not see them together again, with the exception of "pickups and drop-offs," until my college graduation. The next twenty years would see me on the "wit-

> "Anger is a tool for change when it challenges us to become more of an expert on the self and less of an expert on others."
> —Harriet Goldhor Lerner

ness stand," being forced to choose at every crossroad. Mother would declare that if I wanted Dad to come to something significant, like a birthday party or my high school graduation, then she simply would not be attending. Dad would be kind, but could never make it to whatever he was invited to.

Mother was angry, and Dad was absent. Nothing I could do could change that. I couldn't fix our broken family. I cried out, but nobody heard me. Dad started over with a new family. I stood on the outside of my life, watching. I had no voice. Mother couldn't find what she was looking for, and her anger and discontentment grew. When she married for the fourth time when I was in high school, I found words, but they still were not mine. "Congratulations."

When I gripped the steering wheel of my car, two blocks from my house and wailed, I broke the silence. I finally found my voice. I spoke words in a tiny, wounded, six-year-old voice that had been soundless for twenty years. "God, help me," I whispered.

Asking the Right Questions

"Where does it hurt? What happened? Can you put weight on it?" Interview questions get to the heart of the matter. Psychologists tell us that anger is made up of fear, frustrations, and hurt. What are you fearful of? Where have your feelings been hurt? Why are you frustrated?

Good questions will take us right to the heart of our anger. If we answer them honestly, they will help define and clarify the real issue. Is the issue really the trash, or the television, or the laundry? Or is the issue feeling neglected, unloved, or rejected because of the trash, the television, or the laundry? What do the issues represent? Is there a fuel tank underneath them, waiting to be ignited? If it's neglect that we are feeling or rejection that we are fearful of, once we unearth those feelings, it becomes possible to deal with them. The interviewing of yourself is the only way to take your pulse and decipher the real need.

You have to discern what your anger is really about, or you will continue to harm those you love. Unknowingly, you will set them up to be destroyed by your anger. If you say your anger is about the laundry piling up, but you haven't taken your pulse to be sure that that's all it is about, there could be a fuel tank underneath it. Then when your husband disappoints you, as every husband is going to do, he doesn't just get the anger from the laundry, he sets a match to the tank, and it explodes. When that happens, you can't stop the fallout.

> "Don't be afraid to take a big step if one is indicated. You can't cross a chasm in two small jumps."
> —David Lloyd George

The next time you get angry about the laundry, take a few minutes to do an interview. Ask yourself, *Where does it hurt?* "It hurts because I don't feel loved. I feel abandoned in the middle of a lot of work that needs to be done." You have given yourself the opportunity to transform your tone and demeanor from a warrior on the warpath, to a softer, tender woman who feels alone. If your feeling alone still causes you rage, continue digging until you find the fuel tank. Keep the interview going until you get to the soft place of hurt. Chances are good your husband runs from the Indian, but races to the maiden. I'm not saying fake it, I'm saying dig deep enough to uncover what is really there. Underneath all our anger is usually a wounded heart. It is far easier to embrace and comfort a wounded heart than a raging Indian with a tomahawk. If we stay in our anger on the warpath, we will perpetuate the pattern of feeling alone and abandoned that made us angry in the first place.

Part Three

"Why are you afraid to be angry?" my counselor asked me.

"I'm not angry," I answered, somewhat flatly. I would rather lie and still maintain my posture that Christians can handle hard things and not resort to the "lesser" emotions like anger. Lying is much more spiritual.

"If I'm angry then I'm like my mother, and I cannot be that."

"If you are angry and you don't deal with it appropriately and you let it destroy yourself and your relationships, as you are doing right now, then you are like your mother."

"Oh."

I was there to get help. We had gone into counseling to work on several issues in our marriage, most of which I thought were about Paul. Now the counselor was saying I was afraid to be angry? I thought I wasn't afraid to be angry. That's why I would glare at Paul or kick him under the table or say mean things. I thought I was angry enough. But Ken was right. All of those underground behaviors belong to people who are afraid to be angry, who try to couch it or hide it. I spent so much time stuffing and denying my anger that I wasn't paying attention to where it was coming out. I thought I was hiding it, but it was sticking out everywhere. Paul was getting the brunt of it because he was closest to me. Paul, my incredibly patient husband, who knew I wanted to change before I did. God gives good gifts.

My anger with Mother began when she left Dad. It continued as I allowed her to control my life. I was afraid to say no to her. I did what she told me to, but I resented her in my heart. By her fourth marriage, I'd lost respect for her. But I couldn't stand up to her. I still had no voice. I felt completely powerless in our relationship.

Then I became a Christian. That made things better for a while. I tried to sweep all my feelings under the new rug of my faith, but it didn't change my heart. Eventually, I cut off any relationship with my mother. I didn't understand that in cutting her off, I was becoming more like her. My anger grew.

As I met with Ken on a regular basis, I would tell him everything I thought about my anger and why I thought it was affecting me this way or that. Then he would say this, "You're so grown-up and in control. You've told me everything you think, but where are your feelings? Where is the little girl right now in your grown-up world of thinking?"

I would start to cry from my soul. Shyly, she would come. A little six-year-old girl who could only weep. I shed tears for a lost childhood, for parents who didn't love each other, and for my mother and father who didn't know how to love me. I identified with the psalmist who wrote, "Day and night tears have been my food." The previously silent little girl suddenly had a lot to say. She'd never had words before. There are no words for divorce when you are six. Just pain. I realized how completely out of control I felt as a little girl. I

*couldn't stop anything from happening: the divorce, the cus-
tody battle that pulled my loyalty in two, the new families
that both my parents tried to build with new spouses. I felt
helpless and powerless. And I made a commitment, deep in
my soul, that I never wanted to feel out of control, or powerless again.*

Fresh-Brewed Adventures

- Take a long walk with your journal. Find a spot along the way to pray. Ask God to show you the areas of your life that cause rage inside you. Listen to what He says and take notes.
- Start an anger log in your journal. Anger is like a submarine: it's hard to track, you don't know if it's there or when it is going to come up, and it stays submerged until something brings it to the surface. Keeping a log of the surfacing will uncover some patterns.
- Write a letter to someone whom you are angry with. Don't hold any intention of sending the letter; just use it to clarify some of your feelings. Interview until you find the hurt or the frustration or the fear, and write about that.
- Try exercising the next time you get really angry. Take a time-out and go for a run, get on the Stairmaster, or just walk around the neighborhood twice. You will be amazed that physical exertion can clear your head, release tension, and help you calm down.

Where Does It Hurt?

Women will do almost anything to keep from feeling powerless or helpless or rejected. Including hurting others so we
don't have to feel hurt ourselves. We develop a hard exterior
over the top of the wounded place. We fling "You hurt me," as

102

an accusation to be punished. I call that "hard hurt." It reacts like an animal that will bite you when you try to help it. Hard hurt pushes people away and seeks to hurt them in return. We have to move through hard hurt to what is underneath: the tender hurt of the soul. Tender hurt can be soothed, calmed, healed, and dealt with.

The interview process is the only thing that moves me from hard hurt to tender hurt. I have to feel around a bit to discover the wound. "What is really hurting right now?" If I don't give myself space to uncover that, I am quite capable of biting whoever is clos-

"Lord, grant me the serenity to accept the things I cannot change, the courage to change the things I can and the wisdom to hide the bodies of those I had to kill because they really hacked me off!"

—Anonymous

est, whether or not that person caused the pain. Anguish can make us do things we wouldn't do under less stressful situations.

Sometimes you can't even find the tender hurt underneath. The hard exterior has been building for so long, you have forgotten the original hurt. You have gone on with your life, but you have not really healed.

If a leg bone is set properly after a break, it will heal well. Your body, designed by God, is always healing itself. New bone and marrow cells grow, and the leg is as good as new. It's a miraculous thing. But say the bone is not set properly and is just left alone. Or set quickly, but you can't afford the time to be still and stay off of it. Suppose you try to be tough and get through it. Then the miracle of healing becomes a disaster. Growth becomes your enemy as it seeks to heal and reproduce new cells on a broken place, causing more pain and even deformity.

Some of us are limping around on wounds that are decades old. We might not even think they hurt anymore, but they are not healed. Healing at a later stage like this is a hard treatment. The bone must be rebroken and set right. Proper healing is the difference between limping and dancing.

Directed Journaling

- What is your earliest memory of being angry? What is your most recent memory of being angry? Are they related in any way?
- Are you ever dishonest about your anger? Do you hide it? What are you afraid of?

Part Four

I wrote her a letter. It went through four drafts, and the process took a couple of months, but I remember the day I sent it off. I dropped it in the mail slot, and I knew there was no turning back. I also remember that day because I felt love toward my mother for the first time in a very long time.

I invited my mother to come to Nashville to meet with Ken and me. My letter was simple and honest about the road I had been on. I told her about my counseling and that I had come to a place where I felt we ought to at least get together and talk. I wanted to have a relationship with her, I told her, but we needed a new model. What we had in the past was not going to work for me anymore, and if she would be willing to meet with us, we could try to forge a new path.

I really had no idea how she would respond. I was anxious for two weeks. We were traveling, so I couldn't monitor the mail. I had no intention of calling, so I just had to wait. And pray. I realized that I wanted desperately to have a good relationship with my mother, I just hadn't known how. I asked God to work in her life and heart as well as mine.

I stared at the envelope a long time before I opened it. I looked at her distinctive handwriting and wondered what it would say on the inside. She had not responded to me on fancy stationery, just a plain, white envelope and pages from a pad I knew she kept by the phone. It wasn't a long letter, but I knew it was hard for her to write. "Of course I'll come," her cursive read. "I want a better relationship with you more than anything . . . I understand it will be painful for both of us. I do feel if it eases your pain, it'll be worth it to me. I love you, Mother."

I cried as I read her words. She was coming to meet with me on my terms. I was so proud of her. I knew that God must have been working in her life. There was no anger in her response to me, and she was more open than I had ever known her to be.

On June 3, 1994, she met me at Ken's office. It was a time to rebreak the bone. I spoke honestly about the pain of our life together. Over the next three days we wrestled and cried. Our viewpoints weren't always the same. Mother had reasons and hurts that I had never known about. We held each other. She asked for my forgiveness, which I gave freely. I asked for her forgiveness, which she lavished upon me. The bone had been reset, and healing would come.

A period of three days has always had spiritual significance since Christ was crucified, buried, and rose from the dead. Our three days revealed that we had to die to ourselves in order to live to each other again. Like putting our relationship in a cast, Ken helped us set new boundaries that would let our relationship grow straight and strong.

Belgians like their coffee with chocolate.

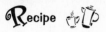

Coffee Malted

Combine 1 cup of double-strength coffee, chilled, in a blender with 2 tablespoons confectioners' sugar, 2 tablespoons chocolate malt powder, and 3 cups chopped ice. Blend until creamy and serve.

Two Good Questions

Anger can make us rush to action, and that is never wise. Anger has done us a great service if nothing other than causing us to take this interview process seriously. If we can sift our feelings before we speak or act, we will be less likely to wound others. We will get our needs met more often than not. The clearest position to move from is one that has been thought through and prayed over rather than rushed into. Rather than "Ready, Fire, Aim!" calling for time to interview can help us shoot straighter.

1. "Am I Compromising Myself?"

Many times when I find myself angry it is because I have not been clear about who I am. Either I didn't stand up for something that was important to me, or I didn't communicate well and a misunderstanding resulted. That doesn't make the anger go away, but it helps me understand where it is coming from and helps me own my part in it.

In *The Dance of Anger*, Harriet Goldhor Lerner admonished us, "In using our anger as a guide to determining our innermost needs, values, and priorities, we should not be distressed if we discover just how unclear we are. If we feel chronically angry or bitter in an important relationship, this is a signal that too much of the self has been compromised."

106

Anger can help us define our boundaries. If my mother calls me at 7:00 A.M. and I am angry when I hang up because she woke me, then I have a choice. Either communicate that I don't want to be called that early, or let it go. If I can let it go, I will; but if I feel compromised, or afraid to ask her not to call, then I am setting myself up to be angry with her over my failure to define myself.

2. "Am I Mad at God?"

"It's essential to own up to how angry most of us are at God for making us live in a fallen world," wrote Hicks and Lee-Thorp in *Why Beauty Matters*. If we believe that God is sovereign, then ultimately our struggle with anger comes back to our relationship with Him. Why did God let these things happen? Why didn't He stop that person from abusing me, or how come He wouldn't help my parents stay together, or did

> "Be angry and yet do not sin."
> —Jesus Christ

He have to allow my mother to die when I was young? Surely if God is sovereign He

could have made certain my life turned out better. And we are angry that He didn't. This question challenges us to bring our anger to the right place. Our husbands cannot handle our "God anger." Our children will not stand under the weight of "God anger." If we try to put "God anger" anywhere but with God, we will annihilate people. Good news: God can handle our "God anger." He isn't afraid of it or of us. If we bring it to Him and wrestle with Him, He will keep it from destroying ourselves. Wrestling with God over issues of anger has been the only way I can discern the purpose of what He is doing in my life.

The Epilogue

Five years of new growth have taken place on the bone of my relationship with Mom. We have something we never had before: a friendship. When I began to write this book, I told her I was going to tell about my journey. I didn't ask for her permission, but I did let her know I was going to write some of our story. She told me to write from my heart and not think twice. "If God can use my mistakes to help others, write every word."

I wrote every word. But I can't leave the story with only the pain. Writing the hard part without telling you a little about my mother today wouldn't let you see the healing. She is not the same woman that I grew up with. Her faith has become alive after decades of dormancy. Her spirit has opened like a morning glory. I have since come to understand more of the pain in her journey. As a little girl I could never understand. As a woman, I can feel the anguish that trapped her.

She is in the seventeenth year of a committed marriage. She is a loving grandmother and an active member of her church. My mother is living proof that it's never too late to begin again. Where I had lost respect, God has restored it. Where before I felt powerless to be myself in her presence, we now spend time on our knees together. Our relationship is not perfect; we still have our days, as we always will, but we are seeking to be honest

> **I don't have a problem with anger!**
> - Are you critical of other people?
> - Are your kids constantly doing something wrong?
> - Does your family frequently ask, "Mom, why are you mad?"
> - Have you broken anything in anger?
> - Does your husband feel praised by you?

with each other and keep short accounts. No more hidden fuel tanks, and no broken bones if we can help it.

We just got off the phone. I had sent her the four parts of this story to read. "You didn't need to send this to me," she said. I smiled. She continued, "You're a good writer." She paused. "Parts of it were hard to read . . . " She took a breath. "But it was good to be reminded how far we've come." I agreed. I hung up the phone, and sat in stillness. Peace, no anger. Healing.

It is impossible to live in this world and not be angry, especially if you are searching for hope and love and real, fresh-brewed life in a world that doesn't have very much to give. This universe is broken and leaves us unfulfilled at times. Coming face-to-face with that truth can drive us to our knees, and it can infuriate us. Facing the pain underneath our anger will enable us to embrace life from a tender, open place. Living honestly and authentically is what we are after, and that does mean getting angry sometimes. But it means dealing with it appropriately. Ask the right questions, raise the hood, tap around a bit. If you find something broken, take the time to set it right. Seek to find the underground fuel tanks, and drain them. Let the healing begin.

SAVOR YOUR
SEXUALITY

Savor: to enjoy, to take delight in

I have been stalling. This is not an easy chapter to tackle.

Just the thought of this cup of fresh-brewed life may send many women running for their footed pajamas. No area of our lives holds as much potential for shame and hurt as our sexuality. In this sex-saturated, intimacy-starved culture, most women live under a blanket of quiet desperation. Lost somewhere between longing and fear, we engage in sex, but wonder if it's all God intended for it to be. We watch with one eye open as the media define sex for us, then we try to deal with our confusion privately. Our churches are conspicuously silent on the subject, offering only enough advice to dismiss any rumors of prudishness. And when we have been wounded, or abused, as one in four of us have, the bewilderment and pain surrounding our sexuality intensify.

I have sat in silence in women's groups while they chatted and giggled about sex on a superficial level, wondering to myself if anybody was telling the truth. I couldn't understand why I had such trouble and pain, so I kept quiet. I have listened to sermons about sex and tried to hide my tears and shame that I wasn't a "better" wife. This chapter will not give you "meet-your-husband-at-the-door-in-cellophane" advice. I will not scold you for not being the sexual goddess of your husband's dreams. What I want to do is encourage you to open the door of your soul and let in delight, true delight, in how you are made.

We can be growing and waking up in all areas of our lives, and our sexuality is no exception. In fact, you may have already found some new life in this area, just from drinking of the previous cups of fresh-brewed life. When we begin to wake up spiritually and emotionally, it can't help but affect us sexually. What affects us in one area of our lives always spills over into other areas.

Our sexuality is a core issue that finds expression in every area of our lives, in the way we dress, the way we speak, the way we walk, the way we engage others, and the way we treat ourselves. Understanding and embracing our sexuality, initially, has nothing to do with any other person. It is the inward acceptance of being created in the image of God and believing that the creation of us is good. We are free to choose how we will express ourselves as we follow the design of God.

"Girls in our culture are caught in the crossfire of our culture's mixed sexual messages. Sex is considered both a sacred act between two people united by God and the best way to sell suntan lotion."
—Mary Pipher, Reviving Ophelia

But forming a coherent sexual identity can be difficult. Between magazine ads, movies, our family values, and our faith, how do we make it all make sense? Who are we, and what are we supposed to be? Let's be honest, there's a lot of pressure to "Be It All!" Especially as Christian women. We want to be the ultimate combination of everything we value. We want to be sexy, but not too sexy. We want to look good, but not too good. We want to be a godly, beautiful, smart, talented woman who cooks, cleans, ministers to the homeless, bakes her own bread, has wild, passionate sex, changes diapers without gagging, teaches a Bible study, works from home, never yells at her children, wears a size four, and lives in a Martha Stewart house! Whew!

That makes me tired.

In trying so hard to be all the things we are "supposed" to be, we end up being nothing that we want to be. Desperately, we dress for others, show up at events we don't want to be at, and try to impress people we don't like. All of us, at one time or another, have defined our sexuality in terms of only pleasing someone else, never pausing to consider ourselves. We barter our personhood through sex, by treating it like something that we do rather than an expression of who we are. As women, it is so easy for us to use sex to get love. But the body and soul are inextricably connected. Sexuality is a soul issue that finds its expression in the body. When it remains only in the body, or when the body is merely used for sexual purposes, there is no real connection, and the soul comes out the loser.

Just Hold Me

What do women really want from sex? I can't speak for our gender as a whole, but most women don't have sex because they want a physical release. Very few women will meet their husband at the door saying, "I am so wound up. The kids are driving me crazy. I have so much physical tension. Everything has gone wrong today. I feel so stressed . . . Could we have sex?" Sex for women is not about function or the physical act. We are after a body, mind, and soul connection. We want emotional closeness—intimacy. We want to feel united on more than one level. This is so important to us, because we were made to connect on several different planes, and when we only

Coffee beans grow at elevations of up to seven thousand feet. Most coffee beans are picked by hand.

connect on one—the physical—we feel cheated. We know there is more, and we want it.

112

Women want passion. We want to be wanted, body and soul. We don't want to be looked at, we want to be "known." Women don't want to be sexy as much as we want to be passionate. Sexy can often be more about how you look, while passion is more about who you are. Someone you don't know or have never met can be sexy but not passionate. Passion comes from who we are. Our whole-bean essence. You cannot know if someone is passionate until you encounter that person's being. This is

> **Things we do to avoid sex:**
> - Stay too busy
> - Pick fights
> - Pretend we are sleeping
> - Have headaches
> - Eat too much
> - Focus on the kids
> - Try not to look attractive

why many women "go away" during sex. They paint the living room or shop at sales in their minds, because nothing is engaging their souls.

Women want to be known. I love that sex in the Bible is centered on this "knowing." I get a thrill reading these words, "And he knew her." One of our deepest longings has the possibility to be touched during physical intimacy, if the emotional, spiritual, and relational pieces are in place. We don't want to be lusted after or used, although too many women will accept those as substitutes. We want to be embraced wholly, as we are, for who we are. We are after a complete knowing, not just sex. It was hard to hide my shock one afternoon at a marriage seminar where we were performing when a woman came up to me and said, "My husband and I are divorcing. I am signing the papers tomorrow. But you know, we've always been good in bed." She must be wired differently than me. It also means that there is more than just sex, or good sex, that makes a marriage work.

If we are bringing who we are to any relationship, how can we share an honest self if we don't have one? Relationships have the capacity to reveal our deepest insecurities. They don't create insecurities, they expose what is already there. Like crazy. We think great sex is just supposed to happen. Chemistry, love, bingo. We've all been to a movie or two, or twenty. But when two flawed, needy, insecure people come together to forge a relationship, it's not always pretty. *Forge* is a word that means brought together in the fire. Marriage brings two separate beings together, to be melted, to form a strong bond as one. Sex plays an important part in making that happen.

Percolations

Books

The Gift of Sex, Clifford and Joyce Penner
Intended for Pleasure, Ed Wheat
Succulent Wild Woman, SARK

Movies

Sabrina (old and new versions)
Sleepless in Seattle
Indecent Proposal (go for coffee afterward to discuss)
A Room with a View

Music

The Mask and the Mirror, Loreena McKinnett
Falling Forward, Margaret Becker
Imaginary Roads, William Ackerman

Our Story

Honeymoon sex is either great or disastrous. We can laugh now, but our first time wasn't great. In fact, I cried. I remember thinking, *That's it?* It's pretty hard to make the shift from taboo to triumph in one night. It's normal for couples to need time to get accustomed to each other sexually. Sometimes it takes months before it gets better.

For us, it didn't get better. I didn't know what was wrong. It took me a long time to admit that I didn't enjoy sex. I couldn't exactly tell Paul. It wasn't him, it was me, but I didn't know why. There was something about it that made me uncomfortable. I couldn't relax. I felt inhibited with no clothes on, and scared. I felt as though I were doing something wrong. When people talked about sex being beautiful, I stared at them as if they were aliens. Ministers talked about the gift of sex, and I was looking for the receipt to take that gift back. I loved Paul, but I didn't love sex. I didn't even like it much.

It didn't take Paul too long to pick up on this. At first I did a pretty good job of hiding it. I had a repertoire of legitimate excuses. But then they started to get old with him. "Do you really have to put that mud mask on your face right before bed?" he would ask me, with pleading in his voice. "Yes," I would assure him, then inside I could relax.

A couple of years in, we began to fight about sex. Our "discussions" became rote. We developed our script and ran it time and time again. The You-Never-Want-to-Have-Sex script. I would feel guilty and give in. But I mostly felt used. I didn't enjoy sex; there wasn't much in it for me. I was afraid I was becoming a robot with no feelings. My mind would wander, but Paul never seemed to notice. Because he didn't notice, I felt alone. I felt that sex was about him and not about me.

> "Let him kiss me with the kisses of his mouth—
> for your love is more delightful than wine."
> —Song of Solomon 1:2

I was getting colder toward our physical intimacy. I struggled deeply with the way I looked. I wanted to take my clothes off about as much as I wanted Chinese water torture. I felt fat and ugly, and I assumed that Paul felt that way about me too. Therefore, he was using me. He would make comments about my sweatpants and wonder out loud why I never wore anything else to bed.

I felt so threatened by other women. If I saw or suspected that Paul was looking at anyone else, I reacted poorly. In the movie theater, or on television, if there was a love scene, I wanted him to avert his eyes. I thought he was comparing me, and I was losing. I imagined my worst fears coming true. I wasn't good enough. I was ugly and fat. He was using me. He wanted other women and not me. What would that say about my worth and value?

One evening I confided in a friend. I didn't know where else to turn. I felt so inadequate to deal with my feelings about my sexual relationship with Paul. This well-meaning friend wanted to brainstorm with me about becoming more attractive. She encouraged me to dress up for Paul and make our sexual relationship "sizzle." I was just dumb and desperate enough to try it. *Sizzle*, I told myself.

I find some comedy in it looking back, but it was painful at the time. I went to Victoria's Secret and bought things. I bought things that I didn't know what to do with! I put several things on backward, and I think they fit better. Talk about self-conscious. Not pretty. Not sexy. Just alone, confused, and angry.

I was back in my sweats in no time, in full rebellion against my own body, not caring about "sizzle." We were surviving in our marriage, but our sexual relationship just limped along. No one to talk to about it. Where are the words? You've got to have some pretty close friends to be able to talk about sex with them, and we didn't.

Eventually this issue of sex, or lack of it, drove us to counseling. Everyone comes to marriage with his or her own baggage,

116

and Paul and I just happen to have issues that accentuate each other's struggles. I thought if Paul could get his life together, everything would be fine. He thought if I could get a handle on my fears about sex, everything would be fine. We both got a wake-up call. "We have met the enemy, and he is us."

Sex became a background issue as we started to unpack our bags. We found anger, abuse, destructive habits, and other problems. I discovered things about Paul that I had never known, and he about me. Sex was revealing the deepest, darkest, most personal struggles we had ever known. It was time to smell the coffee. Our counselor recommended that we stop having sex at all for an agreed-upon time. We stared in disbelief. He said our issues were too intense and we had to deal with them before we could enjoy a sexual relationship without damaging each other.

At first I was terrified of the prescription for us. I thought, *If we don't have sex at all, he is going to despise me.* Paul thought I would be overjoyed at the prospect of not having sex. Which I was. But not for long. Having sex just because it was Tuesday or Friday would have been far easier than doing the work that Ken asked us to do.

Here's what happened.

We had to learn how to communicate and connect. Without sex. We had to reestablish new patterns of relating to each other. Without sex. We had to deal with our family systems and the destructive patterns we had embraced. Without sex. We went to dinner and movies and sat for hours talking. We built a strong friendship. We began to see why sex held the power in our relationship that it did, and how we had misused it. We didn't fight about sex during that time because we couldn't have it. We didn't rush home after a party; we were the last ones to leave. We both were trying to heal and grow up. And the faster the better. We were both motivated.

I'll be honest, it was a long, difficult period. But it changed our lives. It changed our marriage, and it gave us a future that I don't think we would have today had we not done this work.

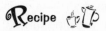

Up-All-Night Coffee Cake

The cake stays up all night, and you can, too, if you like! This is a very convenient cake to make the night before a special weekend breakfast. Either instant or regular pudding mix works well.

3/4 cup chopped pecans
1 package frozen bread dough rolls
1 package (3 3/4 ounces) butterscotch pudding mix, dry
1/2 cup brown sugar
1/2 cup butter, melted
2 teaspoons cinnamon

Butter a 10-inch tube pan or bundt pan. Sprinkle with chopped nuts. Combine dry pudding mix, sugar, butter, and cinnamon. Arrange rolls in the pan. Sprinkle with pudding mixture, distributing evenly. Cover top of pan with plastic wrap and place in a cold oven overnight. In the morning, remove rolls from the oven and preheat oven to 350°. Remove plastic wrap, return rolls to the oven, and bake for 25 minutes. Serves 8–10.

Waking a Slumbering Sexuality

Savoring is going to look different for every woman, but let's go back to our definition of *savor*: delight and enjoyment. What would it take for you to find more delight and enjoyment

118

in sex? If we were speaking honestly, gut level, some of us might say: a new husband, a better body, fewer kids, a different past, clean sheets, an uninterrupted hour . . .

Cherishing Your Body

One of the first challenges I had to face was becoming comfortable with my body. Stopping short of Kathy Bates's support group in *Fried Green Tomatoes* where everyone pulled out mirrors and looked at their own private parts, I had to make some changes. I wasn't pleased with the way my body looked, so I didn't feel comfortable. I began to pray for God to help me be at peace with the way I looked or to help me have the courage to change. God gave me a little of each.

I committed to looking in the mirror again. I wanted to find a home in my body. I "checked out" mentally as often as possible because I didn't like what I saw. I felt alienated and uncomfortable in my own skin. So I would stand in front of the mirror and ask God to help me find beauty there. Even if it was just my eyes or my lips. When I found one thing that I could be grateful to God for, then I would let myself walk away. Sometimes I stood there for what seemed like hours, but I always found one thing. After several times of doing this, the one-things began to add up. I'm not saying that I began to like my body as a whole, but I did find things that I could focus on.

I committed to taking care of myself. I started running to get into better shape. I started slow and didn't run far, but it made me feel great. I am still slow, by the way, but I am training for my first marathon. I would come home after a run, and I would get in the shower or the tub and I would stay for a while, just to focus on my body. I was getting a new shape from running, and it was important for me to notice that. I was starting to respect my body for the way it carried me and for the strength that it was gaining. I bought bath products for "my time" at the end of a run. I found myself shaving my legs because I enjoyed their smoothness. Unlike before, when I would shave only if I thought we were going to have sex, and a little begrudgingly at that. I found a perfume that I liked, and I wore it, without checking with Paul. I wore it because *I* thought it smelled good. Funny, he liked it too.

119

Discovering Delight

I had to learn to play again. I had become so focused on our work and the intensity of travel and "getting the job done," that I had neglected the pure delight of play. When Paul and I were dating, we would play in the leaves in the fall and pick flowers in the spring. We would swim and go to the beach in the summers, and camp and hike in the mountains in the winter. Then we grew up. We forgot that those times were not just recreation, they

> "Every experience of genuine pleasure is fully tasted, not with the connoisseur's boredom born of sampling a dozen wines to know what's best, but instead with the delight that makes this glass the most enjoyable."
> —Emilie Griffin, Clinging: The Experience of Prayer

were spiritual times of refreshing. Without them, we wouldn't know how to delight in our lives.

I searched for a sense of wonder and astonishment in my life. I found very little. Where I discovered it was in the faces of children at play. That's exactly where I lost it. When my parents divorced, I grew up very fast. Work became far more important than play. Grades took precedence over fun five days a week, and Saturdays were for chores. Hobbies were only as good as what they produced, and delight was for the foolish.

Children can lose themselves for hours at a time in pure abandonment of the self to delight. They are captured and captivated by dreaming, imagining, inventing, and creating. I realized I couldn't lose myself in pure abandonment. I held too tightly to everything, my body image, my fear, my need for Paul to "do right," my work. I began to journal about dreaming, imagining, inventing, and creating. I asked God to show me delight and let me lose myself to it.

Relishing Your Senses

If I was disconnected from my body, I was solar systems away from my senses. Intellectually, I knew there were five. Experientially, I couldn't have cared less. I listened, I kept my eyes open, I enjoyed eating, I knew if I touched something hot, and if we passed a skunk in the road, I could make the appropriate face. But the senses were never anything to be relished. They were completely utilitarian. You had to have them in order to function. What a world I was missing. I cannot remember the day it happened, because this sensual awakening was slow, almost as if my black-and-white life was colorized one frame at a time. Running began to wake up my body. Being outside, with nothing to do but put one foot in front of the other, was a new experience, once I got the breathing part down. I had time to look around and notice the leaves on the trees, and the color of the sky, and the gait of the dog in the invisible fence. Smells—honeysuckle and car exhaust. Feel the breeze blowing softly on my skin. Almost taste the freshly mowed grass with wild onions, and the pot roast cooking on a stove top inside. And I could always hear the birds and the crickets, and a still, small voice encouraging me on.

Savoring sexuality as a part of everyday life.
- Be inventive with time.
- Create ambience in your space.
- Take a sexual exploration.
- Find new words for communicating.
- Give the gift of yourself.
- Incorporate play.
- Accept permission from God.

I can't say it was just the running. Everything in my life at that point was conspiring to wake me up. The counseling that I was doing with Paul, abstaining from sex, pursuing creative endeavors in theater, working on my relationship with my mother, draining the anger out of my life (that's a big sense-blocker), and journaling were all very significant parts of my awakening. I began to incorporate my senses into every area of my life. I wanted to surround myself with things that looked good, but also felt good, smelled good, tasted good, and sounded good. Paul and I still weren't having sex, but I was more alive than I had ever been in my life.

Luxuriating in the Spirit

Despising your body simply puts distance between you and your Creator. I had a good relationship with God, but not a passionate one. I was too afraid of passion. Passion sounded sexual, and I didn't want any part of it. But when my spirit opened to my body, my senses, and my new willingness to play, a quickening began to happen in my relationship with God— a dance. With a hus-

> "We can only learn to love by loving."
>
> —Iris Murdoch, Irish writer

band, but without sex, God began to play a more passionate role in my life than ever before. He began to woo me and court me in a soulish way that can only be defined as "a sacred romance." He opened my eyes to see how I had asked Paul to take His place in my life. Paul had become the keeper of my worth. But God was the One who had created me and my body; God was the One who gave me senses to experience; God wanted to be the One to whisper to me of my value. God said if I would look to Him, I could abandon myself and find pure delight. If I were trusting Him to hold my worth, I wouldn't have to fear. If I were trusting Paul to hold my worth, then how Paul lived and how Paul treated me would determine whether or not I lived in fear.

God reached to my core through a book called *Life of the Beloved* by Henri Nouwen. Through it, God called me out of hiding, to claim my identity as His child. He set my feet on the firmest foundation I've ever stood upon: His unfailing love for me. God called me His beloved, and for the first time in my life, I believed it to be true.

Only when we know love can we give love.

Directed Journaling

- Write your sexual autobiography.
- Write a sexual mission statement.
- Write out a sexual fantasy.

Stirrings of Savoring

I was learning to listen to the words of the One who made me. The one true God who wanted to be my God. Caught up in new wonder and mystery, I was changing. But I wasn't changing myself; it was more like the way a caterpillar simply submits to the changes thrust upon him by his God-crafted design. I was becoming who God had called me to be. I was waking up.

For two years we went without sex. I wouldn't advocate that treatment for everyone, maybe not even anyone. I don't know if most marriages could survive it, but ours did. When we brought physical intercourse back into our relationship, it was nothing short of what God designed it to be.

Sex has become a gift for us. Gratitude has a way of changing your perspective. Sex is the gift of ourselves. It is for grown-ups who know the power of one flesh. We made so many mistakes along the way. We wounded each other deeply. I used to wonder what God was doing. What was He thinking putting us together when our issues so totally undid the other? It didn't make sense. But God could see what we could not: we needed each other, but not quite as we imagined when we married. I had a journey toward acceptance of myself and trusting the way God made me. Paul had a journey toward trusting God as well. God used the weakness in the other to push us down a road we wouldn't have walked otherwise.

> "You have stolen my heart, my [beauty], my bride; you have stolen my heart with one glance of your eyes."
> —Song of Solomon 4:9

There's a funny story about a couple in a support group for emotional and physical intimacy in marriage. Every couple had to share how often they engaged in sex with their spouse. The answers varied from once a month to three times a week. In this one couple, the man was smiling from ear to ear. He was just beaming as he answered, "Once a year." The group responded in shock, "Once a year?" Out of the murmurings came the inevitable question, "Why are you so happy?" With a wink and a smile, he quipped, "Tonight's the night!"

My Friend Esther

Sixty-one years old, with a twinkle in her eye bigger than any star, she is one of the most alive, awake women I have ever met. She's definitely fresh-brewed. She exudes the kind of confidence and grace that I can only hope for when I am sixty. What impacts me most is her dynamic sexual relationship with her husband. It's in the little things that she says, the way they look at each other. She's been married for forty years, and the fire is hotter now than it's ever been. I marvel. I smile. I love being around them and watching them. We have vacationed

Slow-brewing coffeemakers release more flavor from the beans.

124

together several times, and they "sneak off" more than we do! She has become my sexual role model. I can see what a healthy sexual relationship looks like, not only right now but into the future as Paul and I grow old together. What an encouragement! When you find couples like that, you must keep them in your life. Have them over for tea and let them inspire you in ways you didn't even know you needed to be inspired. Watch the things they do together. You'll discover their secrets just by paying attention. Here are a few things I've picked up on:

- She takes time for herself.
- They still send each other cards.
- They dance.
- They make time for vacation.
- They do ministry together.
- He respects her immensely.

Every once in a while when we are with these friends, I look over at Paul to see if he is noticing how wonderful they are. He is. He winks at me. We both smile.

Don't give up, dear fresh-brewed reader. Whatever your struggles, and we all have them, whatever the issues in your marriage or relationship, they are not too big for the God who made you. Even if your sexual relationship is good, it can always be better. God will bring healing where you thought there was only brokenness. He will bring comfort where you thought there was only grief. He will bring laughter where you saw anger, and delight in the place of angst. Again, no area holds as much potential for shame and hiding than our sexuality, but to drag those places into the light is to begin the honest journey toward freedom and hope.

As Paul and I both faced our struggles and issues head-on, God brought recovery.

I am much freer today to sit in women's groups and chat about sexuality. I can laugh, where I could only sit in silence before. I make sure the conversation isn't superficial, and I always glance around to find the set of eyes that are holding back the tears. I talk openly about God's hand and healing in my soul and in my marriage.

Learning to savor our sexuality doesn't mean we are seeking to become goddesses, or acrobats, lingerie models, or anything that we are not and it frees us to be that if we wish. It means that we are moving toward being more tender, warm, intimate, inviting, soft, open, and human. We are moving away from being closed, angry, cold, resentful, hard, and rejecting. We will still pad around the house in our ratty robes and sweats. We'll always want to look fresher than we do, but we won't let that stop us from being alive and awake. We'll pay attention to our senses and our bodies. We'll hunt for delight and wonder, and we'll be more open than ever to the God who calls us His beloved.

Fresh-Brewed Adventures

- Take a Five Senses Bath. Light a fragrant candle, put on a tape or CD. Get a fresh-cut flower, and something chocolate or something tasty, and a loofah or mesh sponge to scrub with, and indulge yourself.
- Stand in front of the mirror every morning for seven days and survey your features. You don't have to have your clothes off, but don't leave until you find one thing you can celebrate about yourself for that day.

Seven

CELEBRATE YOUR FRIENDSHIPS

Saturday afternoon at two o'clock. That's what the invitation said. I stared at it daily, my eyes drawn to it like the magnet that held it to our green refrigerator. It was a birthday party for Andrea. For me it was an invitation to a new world. I had never been to Andrea's house, and I didn't know if she had any pets, or cool games, or if she liked the same kind of cake as me, but the possibilities were endless. Mother and I had already bought her gift, a Barbie outfit. I wasn't sure which was harder, waiting to get a gift or waiting to give one. An invitation was a wonderfully tormenting thing. Even if it was like every other birthday party—eat too much cake, watch someone open wonderful presents you wish were yours, run too fast, get a cramp in your side, get too dirty, and head home worn-out with a surprise piece of candy in your pocket and a big Kool-Aid mustache—it would be wonderful. Birthdays were very important parties.

A couple of years ago, my friend Denise gave me the book *Here and Now* by Henri Nouwen. He taught me why birthday parties are so significant: "Birthdays need to be celebrated. I think it is more important to celebrate a birthday than a successful exam, a promotion or a victory. Because to cele-brate a birthday means to say to someone: 'Thank you for being you.' On a birthday we do not say: 'Thanks for what you did, or said, or accomplished.' No, we say: 'Thank you for being born and being among us.'"

This is the heartbeat of celebrating friendship. Rejoicing, honoring, applauding, commending, saluting, toasting the wonderful people in our lives. Not for what they do, but for who they are, and for what they mean to us. "Thank you for being you." Throwing parties over friendship. Not just once a year on a birthday, but as often as we can. Parties in our souls. Gratitude. Celebrating life, the fresh-brewed kind, in a fresh-brewed way, every moment. In friendship, I confess, I am learning from the best. I didn't discover celebrating on my own. I feel celebrated. This chapter of revelry is dedi-cated to three close friends in my life: Audrey, Angela, and Denise. They are soul mates of the first order, and celebra-tors extraordinaire. Friendship is "caught," not "taught," and everything I know, I have "caught" from them. It is a plea-sure to introduce them to you throughout this chapter. They fill a role in my life that no one else can. That's what girl-friends do.

Husbands do not make good girlfriends. Paul is terrific, but he simply doesn't care about the fabric that I like for the sofa. Actually, he does care about the one fabric I like, just not the twenty-four hundred I had to eliminate before I could find the one. That's what friends are for. He doesn't want to know what I think about what everyone is wearing to the Academy Awards. But my girlfriends do. Paul couldn't care less about the cool postcards I found on sale at the bookstore, but I will be in big trouble if I don't call Denise.

Boyfriends don't make good girlfriends. Sounds a bit obvi-ous, doesn't it? But how many of us still try to push the men in our lives into a spot reserved for girlfriends? Don't get me wrong, I have guy-friends, and your husband or your boyfriend should also be a friend, but I'm talking about celebrating the unique role that close female friends play in our lives.

Girlfriends bring out so much in us that no man ever could. They understand us, they cry with us, they shop with us, laugh-'til-we-pee with us . . . no man does that! We are sisters who speak the same language, like the same movies, have similar dreams and goals, and eat more than we should. Vive la friendship! Proximity? Not necessarily.

What determines friendship? Some of the women we see every day we would no sooner call our friends than fly to the moon. Then there are other women that we have met one time but wouldn't call them anything less than a friend. You would think someone who has let you down and hurt your feelings wouldn't make a very good friend. But most of our closest friends have done that. We can all think of people who have never wounded us or disappointed us in any way, and yet we don't necessarily want them for a friend.

So, what determines friendship? Something intangible, that won't be defined. Something inside clicks. Something in our soul responds like a flower opening to the sun. We can't specify it ahead of time, but we know it when we feel it. Friendship is a mystery. The solving of the mystery is impossible. When you ask lifelong friends why they are friends, they can't explain it. "We just are." Then they smile.

If you have one close friend, consider yourself blessed of God. If you have two friends, stand up right now and sing the doxology! If you don't have one person in your life that you could call a backbone, lifelong friend, that means . . . you are probably in the ministry! It could mean you just haven't made a place in your life for a soul mate friend.

When we meet ourselves coming and going, we can't feel the friendship void. How many times have you had a free evening and thought, *Wow, I wish I had one more thing to do,*

130

or another person to try to get together with. Never. We think the opposite. *I'm so glad I don't have to go anywhere tonight!* We imagine the possibility of adding on a friendship, and we're thrilled that we haven't. It's hard enough to carve out personal space, let alone cultivate friendship. Another friend in our lives would just mean more work, and we don't have time for that.

But before long, the void will call again, from a deeper place. On the heels of the evening that we finally have free and we breathe a sigh of relief comes the sight of two friends sitting on a bench conversing deeply, and your soul responds. You want that. As crazy as your life is, you want that. Oh, you rationalize it, and go back to your "I don't have time in my life for one more person" speech. Or you defend it by saying, "I prefer solitude and being by myself," but inside you know that you want meaningful friendship. You were made for it.

Others in your life seem to have satisfying friendships. You see women at Mother's Day Out, or at church, or in the grocery store, talking and connecting, and you feel another twinge. You don't want to need this. Inside, you begin to get angry. Feeling trapped between the demands of your life and your hunger for intimacy, you try to go faster. Your husband is disappointing you at every turn. Without even knowing it, you've placed unrealistic expectations on him to be everything in your life: spouse, lover, friend, god. Your children are cracking under the same pressure. *Why is Mom so mad all the time?*

Relax, the solution is staring you in the face. You need a friend.

You may be saying, "No kidding! I've known for a long time I need a friend, but I can't exactly run to the grocery and get a soul mate." It's true. Most of us aren't looking for just any friend. Life is too busy, and we don't carve out time for anything that doesn't impact us. We want soul mates. We are longing for people or a special person with whom we can pour out our hearts. A safe place where confidences are held care-

"A journey of a thousand miles begins with but a single cup."

fully. An oasis of laughter in the middle of our dry lives. We are on a lifelong interview process to find that handful of people whom we will allow into our lives to call our close friends.

Some women have a group of friends that they have known since grade school. While others, like me, cried out to God for years to bring a close friend. And still others haven't found that person yet. Why do some women have great friendships and others don't? Is it just personality or commitment? Where do you find such friends?

This is Emilie Griffin's answer to that question in *Clinging*: "Don't ask me where such a friend can be found. It is hardly a question of finding at all, for nothing we do can ever accomplish it. To 'find' a spiritual friend is truly to be found, to be chased down, smoked out of one's hiding place in the corner of existence."

So we wait to be found. No one likes waiting, so I suggest celebrating in the meantime.

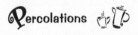

Percolations

Books

The Dance of Intimacy, Harriet Goldhor Lerner

A Garden Path to Mentoring, Esther Burroughs

The Friendships of Women, Dee Breston

Movies

Beaches

Enchanted April

Thelma and Louise

Fried Green Tomatoes

Music

1200 Curfews, Indigo Girls

Along the Road, Ashton/Becker/Dente

Throwing a Party

The good news is, women are instinctively good at parties and at building relationships. Much better than men. A fact that most women take much pride in and tend to gloat over with men, given the right opportunity, like an argument. We know, instinctively, what makes a good relationship and what to do for a fun celebration. We can always tell you what you need to do and why you ought to do it. But that doesn't mean we do it ourselves!

> "Friends don't give friends fruitcakes."
> —A bumper sticker

The bad news is, we also know how to complicate relationships more than men. I can be on the phone for an hour, making plans, deciding on details for a get-together with one of my friends, and Paul can make a call, say ten words, and be out the door! Men know how to keep it simple.

Celebrating your friendships looks just like throwing a party; the elements are the same. Taking my cue from men, here's my attempt to keep it simple with five things you need in order to celebrate your friendships:

1. An Invitation—Time

Angela and I had been casual friends for several years, but we had never spent much time together. Then came this invitation. "I am going to a Christmas benefit, and I would love to have you go with me. I would like to get to know you better."

Getting an invitation to anything is a special occasion. Whether it comes in a phone call, a letter, an e-mail, or smoke signals, the message is, "Your presence is requested." The excitement is undeniable. An invitation piques our curiosity and starts us imagining wonderful things. It doesn't really matter if it's Cinderella at the ball, a dinner at the White House, or

Tuesday morning coffee with your neighbor. We love being invited. Even if we can't attend, it feels good to have been invited.

Every friendship arises out of some kind of invitation. Angela invited me to a Christmas benefit. I invited Denise to look for wallpaper with me. Someone invited me to Audrey's home. Inviting is active. Inviting says, "I was thinking about you, and I am requesting your presence." Inviting says, "I have made time for you and me to celebrate." Inviting makes a hopeful promise of good times.

I look for reasons to make invitations. I'm thinking of designing personal stationery that simply says, "Your presence is requested." Then I can use it for everything I want to invite friends to: birthdays, holidays, Wednesdays, *Seinfeld* reruns, etc. It

> "Acquaintance, n.: a person whom we know well enough to borrow from, but not well enough to lend to."
>
> —Ambrose Bierce

will put me in a constant place of inviting. Occasionally I wake up and think, *Who can I invite today, and for what?* It's almost like a dare.

An inviting home makes a hopeful promise of good times. The minute anyone walks in the front door of Audrey's house, it calls out, saying, "You are welcome here; stay, and spend time." Her home is merely a reflection of her heart. Can we have any higher calling than to invite our friends to that place? To say to them, "You are welcome here in my life; stay, and spend time." What an invitation!

2. A Gift—Yourself

Denise looked at the clock. It was two in the morning. We'd been sitting for five hours on my sofa, completely engrossed in conversation. The flame on the gas logs was dancing, the dogs were snoring, Paul had given up hours earlier and gone to bed,

134

and Denise and I were just getting started. We were going deep. We always do. We don't get together enough to have the luxury of superficiality.

To the party of friendship, you must bring a gift. You've been invited, remember? "Your presence is requested." It would be far easier to bring a kitchen gadget. C. S. Lewis cautions us that we may act kindly, correctly, justly . . . and yet withhold the giving of ourselves, which is love. To offer a vulnerable nugget of your soul that has been mined from a deep, sometimes dark, place is more valuable than gold to your friend.

> I have a friend.
> I sing louder.
> I smile bigger.
> I laugh harder.
> I pray more.
> I love better.

Audrey and I exchange Snow Village pieces every year for Christmas. We try to give each other a piece that embodies the spirit of our friendship that year. Sound silly? Our Christmases have seen doctor's offices, coffee shops, movie theaters, and side-by-side bungalows. Each house or structure says something to the other about who we are. The card of explanation is always better than the piece! This year Audrey gave me Rosita's Mexican Cantina! It shouts of our celebration!

3. Confetti—Encouragement

> "Just wanted you to know I am praying for you. I will always stand in the gap for you, for our friendship, and for our ministries. You are a treasure, my sister. I love you. Press on, Angela."

"A coffee a day keeps the doctor away."

I love throwing things up in the air. At weddings, or on New Year's Eve, everybody wants something in their hands to throw. It's a way of lavishing our love on people. Confetti is a tangible expression of intangible emotions. No celebration is complete without it.

Taking the time to gather little pieces of love, grace, strength, and hope is worth it when you shower your friendships with them. Spiritual confetti! It is the ultimate encouragement.

Angela has celebrated our friendship with this confetti. She leaves amazing voice mails for me when I am on the road. She sends me incredible notes and faxes. When we are together, she prays for me and with me, building me up by her words and example.

Throughout the writing process of this book, each of my friends has blessed me and thrown so much confetti my way. In the midst of my lack of celebration due to neglect, as I write about celebrating, I have felt showered beyond belief. Graced by their free, lavish praise. Encouragement is to a friendship what confetti is to a party. It's light, refreshing, and fun, and you always end up finding little pieces of it stuck on you later.

> "Selfishness is not living as one wishes to live, it is asking others to live as one wishes to live."
> —Ruth Rendell, English writer

4. A Great Cake—A Good Plan and Lots of Laughter

I didn't want just any cake. I wanted something that would hurt people when they ate it. A cake that you want to eat in your swimsuit, so you can dive into it at any moment. (Never mind, forget eating cake in a swimsuit—bad picture!) Anyway, something stellar. When I called the bakery that a friend recommended, I was told I had to place an order two days ahead of time! I was used to walking into the grocery and picking up a cake. For something special, for a real celebration, sometimes you have to plan.

That goes against a lot of you sanguines out there who just like to let things happen as they will. And most of the time that's fine. But every once in a while, when you want to celebrate a friendship, make the plan. Call and schedule the trip, book the tennis court, put together an amazing day. It will communicate loud and clear that you thought about this ahead of time. A good plan can be no plan, if you think it through.

Audrey loves me by planning. When I arrive at her home, I am usually exhausted. She could easily be frustrated by that. Instead, the way she celebrates our friendship is by having a plan. When I am too tired to make decisions, she takes care of every last one. I want to spend time with her and give her all the energy I have. And I have a lot more when I don't have to decide where or what to eat, or what movie to see.

Laughing with friends is just like eating cake at a party. You can have a party without cake, but who would want to? Every friend I have in my life knows how to belly laugh, and not take themselves, or me, too seriously. Laughter is like a tall, creamy, four-layered, beautiful cake that leans to one side. A cake that is meant to be cut and shared. Two forks and enjoyment beyond belief. It feels great to lose yourself in laughter. Doubled over, knees pressed together so you don't pee, face red, tears rolling down your cheeks. Trying to regain composure, getting serious, and then losing it all over again. Celebration indeed!

> "It's the friends you can call at four in the morning that really matter."
> —Marlene Dietrich

5. The Cleanup—Shared Burdens

Real friends are the ones who hang around to help you do the dishes. They aren't the ones who ask if they can help; they're the ones who just get busy. Part of celebrating is cleaning up. When tough things happen in our lives, these friends don't call and ask what they can do. They just do it. Burdens are something that we have to learn to share in friendship, just like letting someone else do our dishes.

Angela, Denise, and Audrey have all done my dishes. In more ways than one. They have carried my burdens on so many occasions. Just a few months ago, I had to let them into the messy kitchen of my life, again. It shouldn't be hard to do that, but it always will be. Each of them, in her own way, rolled up her sleeves and got to work. They never try to "fix" me, or do all my dishes for me, they just stand by my side with their hands in the same dirty water. They aren't afraid of my mess, even when I am afraid to show it. They remind me that they are in my life to celebrate our friendship, from the first invitation through the last dish.

Do a quick inventory of the friends you've invited into your life. Of those that you spend time with, do you have one or more that you could say these things about?

- We mutually share our lives, and we make time for each other.
- We hold each other's personal issues in confidence.
- I could call this person at four in the morning.
- If my marriage was in trouble, I could talk to her about it.
- We'll be friends in twenty years.

Like a Lovely Bouquet

Looking for reasons to celebrate, I uncover gratitude. I realize how much I have to be thankful for. Spending time with my friends allows me to stay in that place of gratitude a little while longer. Celebrating birthdays, victories, answered prayers, and accomplishments lets me savor them before I move on to something else. Throwing a party, even if it's just a cup of coffee shared, is good for the soul.

I am a better wife when I celebrate my friendships. I do my marriage a big favor when I shop with someone else. It lets

Paul off the hook, and it lets me enjoy the time out. I confess, I am not a huge shopper. I never venture out on the day after any major holiday. I don't like having to knock other women down to get the item I want. It hurts my Christian witness. But I do have to buy things, so I do go shopping. And when I do, I want to take my time and enjoy it. But shopping with Paul is like swimming with a shot put. Better to stay out of the pool altogether. So I shop with people I have fun with, which lets Paul do something else.

In addition, I am a more contented person when I celebrate my friendships. I become a better friend. I am blessed that my friends are three women who don't fear one another's presence or position in my life. We don't get together, the three of us; our friendships are separate, unique, and dif-

> "'Stay' is a charming word in a friend's vocabulary."
> —Louisa May Alcott

ferent. Audrey, Denise, and Angela all affirm that I am a better friend to them because I have each of the others in my life as well. Emilie Griffin wrote in *Clinging*, "Because we love this new person, we love more intensely, and more freshly, and with a new immediacy those whom we already love. Love squares and cubes in us."

When we celebrate well, it stays with us, like the confetti we have to brush off our coats the next time we wear them. Audrey has come to the D-FW airport just to have a short visit between my connecting flights. Denise has rearranged her busy corporate workday to take care of some immediate need I might have. Angela has driven two hours to meet me for breakfast when I was in a not-so-nearby city. That's celebration, and we don't forget those things. It puts a spring in our step, a smile on our lips, and gives us a much lighter heart. I can be by myself, five hundred miles from any of them, and something one of

"At the end of the rainbow there's a pot of coffee."

them has said will cause me to laugh out loud. I have expo-
nentially more joy in my life because of them. I bring more joy
to my marriage and to my family because of them. Friendship
fills a deep well within me with fresh water. When I celebrate
my friendships, it's like dropping a huge rock into the well. It
splashes that water everywhere, on everyone else in my life.

139

Fresh-Brewed Adventures

- Celebrate your spiritual birthday, or someone else's. Go on
  a picnic, have a party, or just have a big slice of cake in
  honor of "rebirth." Celebrate being found by God!
- "Request the honor of someone's presence." Practice inviting. Invite your daughter to join you on an errand that you
  normally do by yourself. Write an invitation to a friend to
  meet you for a cup of coffee or tea or lemonade, and give
  her a book, just because. Invite someone to attend church
  or a Bible study with you, and bring cookies.
- Plan an extravagant, expensive, special day with a close
  friend. Think of as many fun things as possible to squeeze
  into one day. Give your friend a copy of the expensive day
  you planned, then do something inexpensive together.
- Next time you are running errands, take a dog with you.
  Even if you have to borrow one. (Mine are available most
  days of the week.) Dogs know how to celebrate. Pick up
  some helpful suggestions from their behavior: hang your
  head out the window, wag your tail when you see people
  you love, enjoy your food, nap anywhere.

Like a Swarm of Bees

Annie Dillard wrote about a young friend that she gets
together with a few times a year:

140

Now she is aware of some of the losses you incur by being here—the extortionary rent you have to pay as long as you stay. We have lived together so often, and parted so many times, that the very sight of each other means loss. The ever-taller embrace of our hellos is a tearful affair, aware as we are of our imminent parting; fortunately the same anticipation cancels our goodbyes, and we embrace cheerfully, like long-lost kin at a reunion.

I feel that way about my long-distance friends. "The very sight of each other means loss." There is so much excitement before a visit, and it seems that I'm not there long before the heaviness sets in. We will have to part, and each of us will be alone again. It seems too high a cost.

Audrey's backyard has a secret garden. She and her husband, Randy, are avid gardeners, or as I call them . . . botanical artists—not by profession, but by love. Much of the longings chapter was written from that wonderful spot, as I tucked myself away amid the flowers and stones. One morning I was listening to the fountain, cherishing the simple beauty surrounding me. Relishing my senses. I complimented her on the lovely flowers that were inspiring me. Audrey told me about her friend who hates wasps and bees. As a result, this friend won't plant flowers in her backyard because she doesn't want the bees. I sat with that for a moment. That's a pretty high price. I relate that to the cost of a long-distance relationship. The parting and pain are the bees, but you cannot have the flowers without them. The beauty of friendship is far greater than the pain of the bees.

"We can do no great things—only small things with great love."
—Mother Teresa

Directed Journaling

- Make a list of special people in your life, from your spouse all the way to the lady at the dry cleaners. Think of some way to celebrate their presence in your life. Even if it's a thank-you and a smile or a special card, find a way to celebrate them. As you write them in your journal, say a special prayer of rejoicing for each of them.
- Are you too busy for meaningful friendship?
- What are some of the dishes (problems in your life) that you need to let your friends help you with?
- Celebrate your friendship with God today.

Keep the Celebration Going

The goal of this cup of fresh-brewed life is not to form an exclusive circle of celebration among your friends. The goal is to celebrate life. To say yes to being more loving, more caring, and more gracious. The choice to celebrate is about us, not about the other person. Like a rock dropped into a well, when celebration begins in your friendships, it will have a ripple effect and touch every area of your life.

Celebrate your family. "We're not friends; we're family!" Whether that is true for you or not, our families are always in need of celebration. Throwing a party, figuratively, can make struggling relationships good and good relationships better. Celebrating says to our families that they matter and they are important in our lives. I am so guilty at times of neglecting family relationships. They are the easiest to take for granted because they're family and because of "scheduled" celebrations like holidays and birthdays. We know we are going to see them eventually, so we don't have to be proactive about getting together. But we miss out on what could happen if we began to invite and encourage and share with them. Our family relationships could develop into some of our deepest friendships.

Celebrate your friendship with God. God, through Christ, has become our friend. Exodus 33:11 says: "The LORD would speak to Moses face to face, as a man speaks with his friend." As you are journaling in the mornings, celebrate your friendship. Have a little party with God. Invite Him to speak to you, bring yourself to Him as a gift, give Him praise, laugh, and share your burdens. Develop your relationship with Him to a new level of intimacy. Your friendship with God is not a stepping-stone to a "real" relationship; it is the cornerstone of all relationships. That we have the opportunity to be friends with God is astounding; that we would magnify that opportunity is celebration!

Celebrate other "connections." Not all friends will be soul mates. There are friends that we "lunch" with, parents of kids who play soccer with our kids, couples friends, and women that we are in a Bible study with. These friends come and go in life, and if one of you moved, you would probably lose touch, with the exception of the Christmas letter. They may not be all that we want ultimately in friendship, but they are definitely worth celebrating.

Why not issue an invitation to a woman you have been wanting to get to know better? Make time to share a piece of cake or a moment of laughter with your next-door neighbor. Your postal worker could definitely use a little celebration. You might be surprised how festive it makes you feel to celebrate others.

You can set the table perfectly, buy a beautiful dessert, open a fantastic bottle of wine, and still not celebrate. Celebration comes from the heart. It is gratitude doing the tango. It is a jack-in-the-box of joy. It is unabashed exultation in the delight of connecting with a friend. Better fried chicken in the company of your closest companions than chateaubriand in the mansion of an enemy. Real celebration cannot be manufactured, nor would you ever want it to be. It is authentic, spontaneous, and deeply spiritual. It is a smile that begins in your soul. Give yourself permission to celebrate your friendships. Let go. Make a big deal over them. Go ahead, fuss a little. You can always go back to humdrum tomorrow. It will still be there. Today, make the most of your fresh-brewed life, and celebrate.

Recipe

(My friend Audrey gave me *The Coffee Book* a number of years ago. All the recipes in *Fresh-Brewed Life* have come from that book. This particular dessert is one of our favorites. We have used every flavor combination of ice cream and frozen yogurt you can imagine, as well as chocolate crusts and graham crusts, and it's always a success. You can't mess this one up! Thanks, Audrey!)

Toffee Ice Cream Torte

1 cup almond macaroon crumbs
2 tablespoons melted butter
1 quart chocolate ice cream, slightly softened
1 cup fudge sauce
1 quart coffee ice cream, slightly softened
4 Heath toffee bars, coarsely chopped

Combine macaroon crumbs and butter, and press on bottom of a 9-inch springform pan. Bake at 350° for 8 to 10 minutes

144

or until golden. Cool. Spread chocolate ice cream evenly on crust; drizzle with half of fudge sauce, and freeze until firm. Spread with coffee ice cream, and sprinkle with chopped toffee bars. Drizzle with remaining fudge sauce. Cover and freeze until firm.

To serve, remove from freezer several minutes before slicing. Cut into wedges with a hot, wet knife. Serves 8–12 (or two good friends for three days).

Eight

Change Your World

Karen finally got the kids down for a nap. Her mother had called with bad news in the middle of putting away the groceries. Her dad was back in the hospital. She was trying to fix something for supper, solve a math homework problem, and find a way to rearrange her day tomorrow to go see her father. Rick was working late for the overtime pay, with Christmas right around the corner. She still had so much shopping left to do. She'd gotten two boxes of decorations down from the attic before she was called away by a neighbor dropping off some cookies. Her life was one endless string of interruptions that felt as long as the lights she still needed to put on the tree—a tree that had been standing naked in the corner for three days. Everywhere she looked were things that were half done. Groceries still on the counter, schedule still up in the air, half-eaten dinner plates on the table, and the cold air coming down from the pull-down space to the attic. I don't have a life, *she thought to herself.* I only have chores and commitments and responsibilities, and I can't even finish those.*

She tried to kick her spirit into high gear. Rick would be home soon, and if she could get the dishes done and the

146

groceries put up and the lights on the tree, it would look like she'd accomplished something. She could never give an account of where all her time went. She knew she'd done all she could, but it never seemed like enough; there was always more that didn't get done. The laundry was piling up, and there were at least two people she was supposed to call, but for the life of her she couldn't remember who. She felt the familiar panic and was about to rush headlong into frenzy mode where she would remain until at least midnight, and then she stopped. She took a deep breath.

Then Karen did something she'd never done before. She put water on to boil for hot chocolate, just for herself. She turned on the CD player and pulled a Christmas disk from the attic box. She stacked some dishes in the sink, and put away the "cold" things from the grocery bags. She got her Bible and sat down in the middle of the Christmas decorations and read Luke chapter 2. She prayed and quieted her ruffled spirit. She had no idea that what she had taken time to do would change her whole world.

He didn't know what he was saying. He told my friend he was looking for another employee. "Someone," he said, "like you, who isn't out to change the world; they just want to do their job." Later, when she told me about it, she couldn't stop the tears. She was hurt, and rightfully so. If you knew my friend, you would know she wants to do her job so she can change the world! And if you saw how competent and professional she is, you would know she *is* changing the world.

Women have a deep desire to create purpose and meaning in their lives. I haven't met one woman yet who said, "I want to look back on my life and realize that it didn't count for anything!" I'm not sure that men understand this about us. They think when it comes to significance that they are the only ones who want to make it count. As if working a high-paying corporate job is the only way to make it count. Implying that changing diapers or trying to get split peas into the mouth of a moving target isn't significant work! I don't think they would appreciate it one bit if their boss stepped into their office about 2:30, took one look at their desk, and said, "Look at this mess! What have you been doing all day?"

Sometimes when asked, "Do you want to change the world?" women reply, "How on earth could I do that?" We are intimidated by the question; we think that changing the world is too big for us. That's better left to someone more talented or articulate. *How could I change the world? There is nothing remarkable in what I do. I raise kids, I drive the car pool; I'm not going to invent anything or influence anyone; I don't wear makeup to the grocery store; I can't even find my car keys . . . Change the world? You've got to be kidding!* But inside, we know we want to.

Creating a fresh-brewed life steaming with significance doesn't just happen. It has to be created. You know as I do that order doesn't arise out of chaos. In fact, order degenerates into chaos in no time. If we simply let our days "run their course," we will find ourselves asleep and missing out on real life in no time. It is much easier to react to what

> "Our deepest fear is not that we are inadequate. Our deepest fear is that we are powerful beyond measure. It is our light, not our darkness, that most frightens us. We ask ourselves, 'Who am I to be brilliant, gorgeous, talented and famous?' Actually, who are you not to be? You are a child of God."
> —Nelson Mandela

happens than to take bold steps toward change and purposefulness.

I love the story of the woman who cut the end off a ham before she cooked it. When asked by her husband why she was cutting the end off a perfectly good ham, she replied, "Because that's the way my mother did it." Later, she asked her mother why she cut the end off the ham every time she cooked one. Her mother confessed, "I'm not sure, but it's the way my mother did it when I was growing up. Maybe it had something to do with their health back then." The mother, several weeks later, remembered the question and out of curiosity asked her mother, "Why did you always cut the end off the ham before you cooked it?" The grandmother didn't miss a beat. "I had to make it fit the pan!"

Are you changing the world, or is the world changing you? Are you cutting off pieces of your life for no good reason? We don't have the same pans that our grandmothers did. We have opportunities and choices they never had. We can keep the whole ham and feed a few more people while we're at it!

Let's drink this cup of fresh-brewed life in five sips.

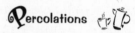

Percolations

Books

The Path, Laurie Beth Jones
Half-Time, Bob Buford
The Life God Blesses, Gordon MacDonald

Movies

City Slickers
The Fisher King
Awakenings
Forrest Gump

Music

Soundtrack from *Les Miserables*
Where I Stand, Twila Paris
Joy in the Journey: Michael Card's Greatest Hits

1. Multiply Your Talents

Have you ever found yourself thinking, *What I do doesn't really matter. Nobody lives or dies based on how many loads of laundry I do today* (well, maybe your husband's coworkers do). *What difference does it make if I show up for work or not?* We think that our donation to life couldn't be very significant. *All I do is clean up after people and cook meals.* We reduce our own contribution. *I don't make much money. I'm not in the ministry, and I don't see myself becoming a missionary.* We convince ourselves that finding no meaning, passion, or purpose in our lives is normal. *This is just the way it is. I should be happy.* Wake up!

Sometimes we don't want others to notice our accomplishments. We downplay everything. We worry what people might think if we are good at what we do. *She is just trying to get attention. She really wants power or prestige; that's not godly.* So we shrink, and we never dare to attempt great things. *What are you thinking? Trying to write a book. You could never do that.* We say, "Not me, I couldn't." Out of fear, we miss what God is calling us to do, or worse, we refuse to do it. And *that's* not godly. Wake up.

Remember Jesus' parable of the three people who were given a different number of talents to work with? The master gave one man five talents, another man two talents, and yet another just one. When the master returned, he wanted to see what each had done with what he had given them. The first two had multiplied their talents in different ways but were able to show the master something for what he had given them. The last fellow confessed that he had hidden away his money because he was afraid.

I used to think this parable was about success. How to make the most of what you've been given. And in some ways I suppose you can still look at it that way. But for me, this story

After petroleum, coffee is the second largest commodity in the world.

150

has become a living lesson about fear. Don't talk about all the great things you are doing when there is a deeper question. What are you not doing in your life that God is calling you to do? Do you stay busy so you don't have to do what God might be asking you to? So many women I know have dreams of writing books, or starting companies, or getting more involved with a particular ministry, but they don't do it because they are afraid of failing.

We've had so much criticism in our lives that we don't try anything new because we fear we'll get it wrong. That fear might manifest itself in a critical spirit of other people's work.

> "Nothing fails like success because we don't learn from it. We only learn from failure."
> —Kenneth Boulding

What's the big deal about writing poetry? I could write that, anyone could. But you don't write because you're afraid.

Sometimes we don't use our gifts because we're afraid of succeeding. If you launched out to start a magazine, and it was successful, it could change your life. You would then have to face new challenges. How could I have a hot meal on the table if I can't get home from work until 5:30? So you don't do anything.

This parable cuts to the heart of that fear. The Scripture doesn't tell us that the first two men in the story did everything right. Each of them "won some and lost some," but at the end of the day, they gained because they used what they had.

Are you tightly clutching what you have? Afraid to let the world see the gifts God has given you because they might not embrace them or understand them? Maybe the fear of losing control has you burying your talent. Bob Buford, in his book Half Time, wrote, "In tossing aside the security blanket which has kept you safe and warm . . . you may feel, at least at first, like you are losing control of your life. To which I say: Good for you."

I got to know Terry Willits this year as part of a women's conference in which we both were leaders. Terry is the author of *Creating a SenseSational Home* and *Simply SenseSational Christmas*. She is a wonderful speaker and a passionate voice for Christ. Her message of using your home to create impact in your world has changed my world and my home along with thousands of other women's homes. Here's what's so special about Terry: she is using her gifts in complete obedience to God. Terry wants to be a mom. She would rather be home raising a family, creating a SenseSational life. But God hasn't blessed Bill and Terry with children, yet. She travels and speaks, not because she wants to, but because God has called her to. Her gifts are employed in His service, and this is where He is telling her to use them. She is not unhappy. Terry is a beautiful, joy-filled woman, but if she were in charge of planning her life, it would look different.

> "Character cannot be developed in ease and quiet. Only through experience of trial and suffering can the soul be strengthened, vision cleared, ambition inspired, and success achieved."
> —Helen Keller

Tim Keller, the senior minister at Redeemer Presbyterian in New York City, recently asked this question: "Did you buy in to Christianity to serve God or to have God serve you?" Are you willing to use what God has given you to radically impact this world? Or do you think it's better to stay calm, hide our gifts, and never rock the boat?

Not only is God calling us to rock the boat, He's calling us to get out of the boat! Each of us as women has a mandate on our life to make a difference in this world. Not because we're women, but because we're Christians. That difference at its core is not about what we do, but about who we are. I believe we are called to use our gifts to leave this world better than we found it: with more love, more forgiveness, more hope.

2. Get Control of Your Schedule

We were sitting in a villa in San Diego on vacation when my friend Gail asked me, "What do you want written on your tombstone?" I was taken aback. I had honestly never thought about it. That was two years ago. I haven't stopped thinking about it since.

That question knocked me over. It still does. If you could stand around your own funeral and hear people talk about what they remember about you, what would you want them to be saying? *Great friend, wonderful wife, committed Christian, talented actress . . .*

The tombstone asks a far deeper question than, "What did you do in your life?" It asks, "What did you do *with* your life?" This question gets to the core of who we are and what we value. This question is as important for a stay-at-home mom as it is for the president of a Fortune 500 company.

Bob Buford wrote, "An epitaph should be something more than a wispy, wishful, self-selected motto. If it is honest, it says something about who you are at the essence of your personality and your soul."

An epitaph is very "big picture." It seeks to capture the most important aspect of your life. Since these words are not etched until after you are dead, they are usually written by someone else, someone who looks at your life from the outside. All they have to go by many times is what you "did" and how you spent your time. This is why it is so critical to get control of your schedule—to let who you are come out in what you do. People may look at your calendar of activities and completely miss what you would want them to see.

When we are honest, most of our days are full of things that we really don't want to be doing. It is hard to find epitaph material in those activities. What woman in her right mind would want carved in stone above her head, "That Woman Could Iron"? If the deepest, most prominent desire of her heart is to be remembered as a loving, caring mother, then ironing takes on an eternal significance that it didn't have before, but it isn't enough by itself. Unplug the iron, and get on the floor with the kids and play. Making ham sandwiches becomes the holy pursuit of your passion, but it is only the means to the end. You can get lost in bread and mayo and miss the real meat.

Time is your enemy when it comes to changing your world. Little things that you never have "time" to do yield the biggest results: a conversation with your neighbor, a Yahtzee game with your teenager, taking food to a sick friend's family, reading with your child. When we let our "schedules" consistently get the best of us, we do not have impact. We will never get it all done. There will *always* be plenty to do. There is

> "From most of history, Anonymous was a woman."
> —Virginia Woolf

always more ironing, more cleaning, more phone calls, more business travel, but special moments with your children or opportunities to help someone in need might not come around again.

I love what Lee Iacocca said about this:

I'm constantly amazed by the number of people who can't seem to control their own schedules. Over the years, I've had many executives come to me and say with pride, "Boy, last year I worked so hard that I didn't take any vacation." It's actually nothing to be proud of. I always feel like responding, "You dummy. You mean

154

to tell me that you can take responsibility for an $80 million project, and you can't plan two weeks out of the year to go off with your family and have some fun?"

It is easy to be critical of our husbands for not spending enough time with the kids or at home, but we can find ourselves at home not spending time with the kids either. Controlling your schedule doesn't necessarily mean that you are home a lot or that you have large chunks of time with nothing to do. That won't necessarily help you change your world. The only thing that will change your world is your desire to change it, but keeping a rein on the calendar will help to make that a reality. The calendar answers to you, as opposed to you answering to it.

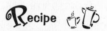

Recipe

Frozen Espresso Mousse

1 tablespoon instant coffee
1 tablespoon hot water
4 eggs, separated
1/2 cup sugar
1 cup whipping cream
3 tablespoons Kahlua

Dissolve coffee in hot water and set aside. Beat egg yolks until thick and lemon-colored. In a separate bowl, beat egg whites until stiff, adding sugar gradually until glossy. In another bowl, beat cream until stiff. Blend in coffee mixture and liqueur. Fold all three mixtures together gently to combine. Pour into a freezer-proof container. Cover and freeze. To serve, scoop into small bowls. Serves 4–6.

3. Find the Passion That You Live and Die For

What does it profit a woman to gain the whole world if she loses her own soul? Or in my language, "Do I win if I complete all the tasks, but lose my sanity in the process?" I am a Superwoman wanna-be. I have put my résumé in three times, but haven't gotten the job (it's probably those dang tights). I say yes to almost everything. I believe that I can work miracles, and sometimes I can. But nothing robs my life of meaning faster than simply saying yes to doing something that my heart is not in. The amount of work we do has nothing to do with the impact we are having. Significance does not come from doing more. Burnout, crabbiness, lack of gratitude—all of these things come from doing too much. We don't change the world by taking it all on. Those who know me are going to

ask if I'm reading my own book. And I will when I get time.

Between supper, baths and bedtime, or meetings, phone calls, and commuting, what woman

> "Faith is not making religious sounding noises in the day time. It is asking your inmost self questions at night—and getting up and going to work."
>
> —Mary Jean Irion, Yes, World

has time to think about meaning? With the complete loss of free time as it is, how can we be talking about doing more or taking on something else? Susan Douglas wrote in *Where the Girls Are*, "Study after study shows that while working dads have time to read the paper, watch guys with arms the size of Smithfield hams run into each other, go out with boys for a frosty one, or simply take a nap, working moms barely have time—or the opportunity—to pee with the bathroom door fully closed."

If we can't pee with the door closed, how in the heck are we going to change the world? First, relax. Pursuing significance or seeking to change your world doesn't necessarily mean

156

taking on anything new. It might mean doing an analysis of your gifts and getting control of your schedule and then listening to God. Go back to your epitaph. How do you want to be remembered? What motivates you to work? This passion that we are looking for is not the "what" so much as it is the "why." Dream a little bit. Okay, dream a lot. If you could have any life in the world, whose would it be and why? What gets you out of bed in the morning? It may be slow, but it still motivates you. Is there something that God is calling you to do? Have your journal out and just listen. Then write down what He tells you.

I have a friend who says, "The deepest question of our lives is not 'If you died tonight, do you know where you would spend eternity?' That's a good question, and one that must be settled, but the deeper question is 'If you wake up tomorrow, do you know how you will spend the rest of your life?'" A lot of us aren't afraid of dying. We're afraid of living. We don't know what we are living for. We know that Jesus will be there for us when we die, if we have a relationship with Him, but we don't understand what kind of life He is calling us to today.

> "All serious daring starts from within."
> —Eudora Welty

There is something that God is calling you to do. You know it. You've always known it. You may not know exactly what it is, or what shape it will ultimately take, but it is unique to you and it is why you were put here on this earth. I don't think this passion is just handed to us like a gift. I think it is revealed in us over time like an excavation. Everything extra gets chiseled away. Bob Buford writes about this "one thing" that we are seeking to discover in *Half Time*. "All I can tell you with any degree of certainty is that you will not find an abiding sense of purpose and direction by rushing from business appointment to church meeting to your son's soccer game to dinner with friends and then to bed. If you cannot afford to take the time and solitude before God that finding your 'one thing' requires, you are not ready to find it."

Finding your passion is the single most important ingredient for changing your world. It's like yeast in bread—without it you will have flat, hard dough. Uncovering God's purpose in your life and following it will lead you to the greatest satisfaction there is. When we work out of our God-given passion, we get tired, but not weary. We need rest, but not a change.

Many women don't think they need passion. They just work. They've defined God's will as the hardest, worst thing they can think of to do. They complain the whole time. There is no joy in their lives; no "change-the-world spirit," just an angry expectation of brownie points in heaven for taking the hard road and a life that's as stale as two-day-old coffee.

Directed Journaling

- Make a list of phrases that you would love to hear people say about you at your funeral.
- Start thinking about what you want written on your tombstone.
- What gifts has God given you that you aren't using for Him?
- If you wake up tomorrow, will you know what you're living for? What is your passion, your "one thing" that you want your life to be about?

4. Stop Waiting for Your Life to Begin

Say this with me out loud: "The quality of my life is determined by one thing: my attitude toward it." Say it again. "The quality of my life is determined by one thing: my attitude toward it." One more time . . .

158

A number of years ago our travel schedule intensified beyond my threshold of comfort. That is a nice way of saying I burst into tears and chained myself to the bed before each trip. I would find myself praying, "Father, just help me get home and back to my life." I began to see our work and travel as an interruption to my *real* life. I would put my life on hold while we were traveling and wait until we could get home to resume life. Then one trip changed all that. God interrupted my "let me get home" prayer to tell me that for now, traveling was my life, and I could choose to miss it or I could embrace it. My eyes were opened, and I realized how much I had been missing on the road. We had the opportunity to see the world, and I was missing great things about every city we went to. Traveling began to take on an adventurous quality for us. Finding a great restaurant or going to the zoo or stopping at an art museum became a way to enjoy more thoroughly the life that God had called us to.

Find the meaning in today. Don't miss the life that is in front of you. Sarah Ban Breathnach wrote in *Simple Abundance*, "If I do not endow my life and my work with meaning, no one will ever be able to do it for me." Your attitude determines how much you enjoy your work. If you don't think enough meaning exists in your life, create it. Don't just run errands; use the opportunity to meditate. Pray for the businesses in your community you have to visit. Your bank and your dry cleaners both could use your prayers. You are on God's agenda now. He has given you meaning and purpose; splash in it. Don't just eat a quick bite; "dine instead." Even if it's peanut butter and jelly by yourself. Take it outside, savor the taste, enjoy the moment, breathe in the beauty. Celebrate the significance and wonder of life. Don't wait until it hits you over the head. It's already there; embrace it.

Getting the house ready for Christmas is a great example of this. I try to "get through" decorating and miss the joy of the process. We stay up until midnight to get the decorations "just so" and we can be gripey and joyless in the process. Instead, put on the Christmas music and the hot chocolate and get to work, but don't miss the specialness of the moment. So your tree is not on a magazine cover; if you connect with your family and enjoy the process, isn't that what it's about? The joy of the spirit of Christmas is begging to overrule the chaos. Give in and let it.

Look for the extraordinary in the ordinary. Just in your short or long drive to work, think of all the things you pass, yet don't notice every day. Someone crying in the car next to you, the sunrise, a cornfield bringing forth firstfruits, the new shrubs in the neighbor's yard. Opportunities to minister, chances to have your breath taken away by beauty, a great idea for a new business. Missed—all for listening to the radio and paying half attention.

I was getting a cup of coffee and a bagel in Colorado Springs last week. I commented to the waitress that I hoped she had a good rest of the day. "How can it be good when I'm working?" she asked. I told her, "Don't postpone your life until you get off. Just think about at work what you would think about if you weren't working." She smiled and then laughed. "I guess I could do that." Sure she could, and so can I. The quality of my day is determined by one thing: my attitude toward it.

Can you have a good day if you have to work? Can you allow yourself to enjoy even the most mundane tasks simply because it is the work that has been given you for the day? If you can't, you are giving your work, a task, or even another person too much control over your life. If you let your soul bubble over while you are working or doing something that is unpleasant to you, you are living a fresh-brewed life, and you

The first Parisian cafe opened in 1689 to serve coffee.

160

can't help but change the world. It is changed by your presence and by your complete freedom to live at a place different from where most people live. It is our relationship with God that sets us free. We know that our happiness isn't dependent upon other people or circumstances.

To close this section I'm including a piece I came across last year. It speaks to this issue of waiting for our lives to begin. It touched me deeply.

A Story to Live By
by Ann Wells (*Los Angeles Times*)

My brother-in-law opened the bottom drawer of my sister's bureau and lifted out a tissue-wrapped package. "This," he said, "is not a slip. This is lingerie." He discarded the tissue and handed me the slip. It was exquisite; silk, handmade and trimmed with a cobweb of lace. The price tag with an astronomical figure on it was still attached. "Jan bought this the first time we went to New York, at least 8 or 9 years ago. She never wore it. She was saving it for a special occasion. Well, I guess this is the occasion." He took the slip from me and put it on the bed with the other clothes we were taking to the mortician. His hands lingered on the soft material for a moment, then he slammed the drawer shut and turned to me. "Don't ever save anything for a special occasion. Every day you're alive is a special occasion."

I remembered those words through the funeral and the days that followed when I helped him and my niece attend to all the sad chores that follow an unexpected death. I thought about them on the plane returning to California from the Midwestern town where my sister's family lives. I thought about all the things that she had done without realizing that they were special.

I'm still thinking about his words, and they've

changed my life. I'm reading more and dusting less. I'm sitting on the deck and admiring the view without fussing about the weeds in the garden. I'm spending more time with my family and friends and less time in committee meetings. Whenever possible, life should be a pattern of experience to savor, not endure. I'm trying to recognize these moments now and cherish them.

I'm not "saving" anything; we use our good china and crystal for every special event—such as losing a pound, getting the sink unstopped, the first camellia blossom.

I wear my good blazer to the market if I feel like it. My theory is if I look prosperous, I can shell out $28.49 for one small bag of groceries without wincing. I'm not saving my good perfume for special parties; clerks in hardware stores and tellers in banks have noses that function as well as my party-going friends'.

"Someday" and "one of these days" are losing their grip on my vocabulary. If it's worth seeing or hearing or doing, I want to see and hear and do it now. I'm not sure what my sister would have done had she known that she wouldn't be here for the tomorrow we all take for granted. I think she would have called my family members and a few close friends. She might have called a few former friends to apologize and mend fences for past squabbles. I like to think she would have gone out for a Chinese dinner, her favorite food. I'm guessing—I'll never know.

It's those little things left undone that would make me angry if I knew that my hours were limited. Angry because I put off seeing good friends whom I was going to get in touch with—someday. Angry because I hadn't written certain letters that I intended to write—one of these days. Angry and sorry that I didn't tell my husband

and daughter often enough how much I truly love them. I'm trying very hard not to put off, hold back, or save anything that would add laughter and luster to our lives.

And every morning when I open my eyes, I tell myself that it is special.

Every day, every minute, every breath truly is . . . a gift from God.

ℱresh-Brewed Adventures

- Get out your good china, wear your favorite blazer, spray your best perfume, and run errands. Have a party with your loved ones because you can. Stop postponing your life.
- Try a "Receiving Praise Week." Anytime anyone gives you a compliment, just receive it. No ifs, ands, or buts—just a simple thank-you, period. If any notes of encouragement come your way, take them to a special place, receive them, and thank God for them.

---

5. Learn to Receive Praise

Why are we so afraid of accepting kind words? We deflect them and do anything we can to let them bounce off us rather than take them in. We think it's more spiritual to do that. However, when we receive words of criticism, we take them right to our core. Why do we do that? Do we really believe it is more holy to let critical words into our soul while praise stands outside in the cold? We need to learn to receive the praise we have been given. SARK had this to say: "Do you actually know anyone who got a 'swelled head' from too much praise? Usually it was far too little, and they retreated to their ego for escape and became grandiose as a type of defense."

A number of years ago, a friend working in our office res-

With the exception of Hawaii, no coffee is grown in the United States.

cued from the trash several thank-you notes about performances we had done. "Why are you throwing these away?" Cindy asked.

"I don't know why I would keep them," I replied, embarrassed. *What do you do with a letter telling you how wonderful you are after you've already read it?* "It feels a little self-centered."

"Let me keep them for you," she answered. "You might want them one day."

"Whatever." So, when the mail brought a special note, I would read it, thank God for using us, and pass it on to Cindy. She began a file in our office called "Applause."

That file still exists. Whenever we get a kind or encouraging note or letter or newspaper article or review, it goes into that file. There have been some hard days in our eleven years of performing. Days where I have wondered if we are making a difference or if what we do really matters. I have sat quietly with that file open on my lap, tears flowing, grateful that Cindy taught me how to receive praise.

Spiritual anorexia is refusing the things, like praise, that will nourish your soul. It's a control issue. Women are starving for affirmation, encouragement, and praise. We are so thirsty for someone to think that we are doing a good job at something, anything. Yet we turn down praise because we think it will make us arrogant if we accept it, or that we will become indebted in some way to whoever is thanking us. This is a flawed view of praise that reflects insecurity in our true identity. You cannot change your world if you won't allow people to thank you. You will never believe you are making a difference.

Here's what I do. Say thank you, and take it. Don't deflect it and act as though it were nothing. Don't try to pass the glory off to God . . . yet. Just receive it. Don't dismiss it or trivialize it or wave it away. Accept it. Take it into your soul and allow it to nourish you. Then later, sit with your encouragement. Take the note or the gift that you've been given, or the words of the compliment to a quiet place. Then prayerfully and thankfully acknowledge your Creator. Give Him the praise that was given to you. Hand Him the glory that someone handed to you. Then save it. Put the card in a special place or write the words you were given in your journal. Next time you are feeling discouraged, go to that place and allow God to remind you that He is using you to change your world.

Seeking to live a fresh-brewed life will change your world. As you multiply your talents, the aroma of God's gifts to you will begin to waft toward others. When you get control of your schedule, the warmth that you have to share will wrap around your home and your loved ones. And when you discover and embrace the passion that God has created in you, your neighborhood and your community will feel the impact. You can't stop it. It isn't you; it's Him. He is drawing people to Himself and changing the world through how He made you. This is life. Here and now. Not when we have everything that we want, or when all of our questions are answered, but today. And when the world begins to wake up alongside you, and they begin to thank you for being authentic, just smile and say thank you. Then get on your knees, and praise God for a fresh-brewed life.

ENRICH YOUR RELATIONSHIPS

She stood at the altar, dressed in white, a vision of pure loveliness. When the minister asked the bride the most important question, she softly whispered, "I do." She squeezed his hand and looked at her intended lovingly. He smiled. When asked the same question, the groom replied, "I do." She turned to him and said, "Why did you say it like that?"

The hardest part about relationships is being in them. If we could look at them from the outside with our faces pressed against the glass, we would all be relationship experts. It is a piece of cake to be a relationship expert on someone else's relationship. We know exactly what they should do and why they should do it.

It's the same way with raising children. Everyone has advice for you. Charlie Shedd wrote about teaching the Ten Commandments of raising children. Then he had children. His list became Ten Good Things you ought to do when you raise children. By the time they were teenagers, he had Ten Suggestions if you ever have kids.

Women are relationally gifted. God has given us the ability

166

to see things that men simply don't have eyes to see. Gary Smalley believes that women have a built-in understanding of relationships that men don't have. It's an internal manual. We know what will make a bad relationship better. We are blessed with an ability to nurture and meet needs in a way that men can only dream of.

But knowing and doing are two separate things.

It's one thing to talk about insecurity in relationship; it's another thing to feel insecure. It's incredibly easy to teach about forgiving others; it's excruciatingly painful to forgive. What could be more simple than extolling the virtue of good communication? Yet communicating honestly continues to be a huge issue in our relationships. Knowing what to do is easy. It always will be. Doing it is the real challenge.

> "Good communication is as stimulating as black coffee, and just as hard to sleep after."
> —Anne Morrow Lindbergh, American writer and aviator

What can move us from understanding to practicing? What can keep us from reading this chapter, or anything on relationship, and saying, "I know this"? The truth is, we do know this. We "know" too much. We know our way into jealous rages, critical spirits, bitterness, destructive patterns, affairs, and divorce.

To know will never change us. Not in this culture. We have so separated knowledge and experience. We have driven a wedge between understanding and embracing. You can know everything and do nothing.

For fun, I looked up the word *know* in my thesaurus. Here's what I found: understand, think, comprehend, discern, fathom, grasp, look at, notice, observe, perceive, realize, recognize, see, take in, view, espy, assume, conceive, estimate, gather, imagine, infer, suppose, and suspect.

Guess what? You can understand, think, comprehend, discern, and fathom without giving. You can grasp, look at, notice, observe, and perceive without caring. You can recognize, see, take in, view, espy, and assume without ever loving. And it's not a problem to conceive, estimate, gather, infer, suppose, or suspect without ever doing anything.

Perhaps this is why our relationships are in such trouble. Henri Nouwen wrote, "While the desire for love has seldom been so directly expressed, love in its daily appearance has seldom looked so broken. While in our intensely competitive society the hunger and thirst for friendship, intimacy, union, and communion are immense, it never has been so difficult to satisfy this hunger and quench this thirst."

We "know" too much. We are on a quest for knowledge. We read too many books and watch too many talk shows and hear too many sermons without putting one thing into practice. Knowledge is killing our relationships. At the end of the day, after two talk shows, a Dobson program, and a conversation with your "know-it-all" neighbor, when you've yelled at your kids, or said mean things to your husband, or forgotten to celebrate your friendships, ask yourself this question: "What principle will ever change my life unless I do it?"

Knowledge is not the key. Knowing the principles profits us nothing. Not when it comes to relationships. It is not enough to know. There must be a responsibility to knowledge. Some weight, some commitment, something more.

In my thesaurus I came across one word that stopped me. In all the grasping, comprehending, noticing, perceiving, there is a word that doesn't fit. There is one word for *know* that called me to more: *trust*. This is the bridge. Trust is what makes knowledge count in relationships. If our knowing is moving us toward trusting, then it is helping. Otherwise, it is only knowing. You can't trust your way to divorce. You can't trust your way into a jealous rage. You can know that you shouldn't feel insecure about your friendship, but you can't trust your way to insecurity.

168

Trust will wake us out of our knowing into doing. It forces us to let go. Trust is like faith. You cannot see it; you just do it. All the knowing will not produce it. It must be given. Here are some other words from the thesaurus for *trust*: confidence, belief, credence. To trust is to "depend on, rely on, bank on, build on, count on." You cannot trust without moving out of your head. You cannot depend on someone or build on something with mere knowledge. The soul must be part of the equation. The words call us to action, not inspection. The word *on* is significant as well. You can't merely rely. You can't depend by yourself. You can't build in air. There is a requirement of someone or something else that moves us out of our selves.

> "Sometimes I wonder if men and women really suit each other. Perhaps they should live next door and just visit now and then."
> —Katharine Hepburn

We can know, yet not do. We can gather facts, and give nothing in return. We can observe all day long without ever caring. But we do not trust if we don't care. We do not give to something if we don't trust it. And if we say we trust the truth, and yet do nothing with it, it reveals we have not trusted it at all. Trust requires something of us. Trust holds the feet of knowledge to the fire of action.

> *Enrich: to make richer by the addition or increase of some desirable quality, attribute, or ingredient*

We've sipped eight cups of fresh-brewed life thus far. Each previous cup had less to do with others and more to do with ourselves. You embrace your beauty without waiting for someone else to embrace it first; you encounter your journal whether anybody pats you on the back or not; you interview your anger for what it teaches you, then you learn to apply it to your relationships.

This chapter is a closer look at how living a fresh-brewed life will enrich your relationship with your spouse or boyfriend. We'll look at each of the cups that we have sought to draw from and incorporate their truths into the realm of our relationships, to enrich them by increasing this desirable quality: trust. Enriching our relationships with trust is like adding vitamin C to orange juice, or fortifying milk with vitamin D. It provides more nourishment and enhances what is already present.

This is the invitation to move beyond "knowing" the principles of waking up to trusting them to work for you; to learning to trust others with what you are experiencing in your life; to move from understanding a fresh-brewed life to living it out in the presence of those we love.

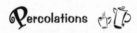

Percolations

Books

    Relationships, Les and Leslie Parrott

    The Mystery of Marriage, Mike Mason

    Love Is a Decision, Gary Smalley and John Trent

Movies

    Sense and Sensibility

    When Harry Met Sally

    While You Were Sleeping

    Much Ado About Nothing

Music

    Lead Me On, Amy Grant

    How Did You Find Me Here, David Wilcox

    Jim Croce's Greatest Hits, Jim Croce

Enrich Your Relationships by Continually Giving Yourself to God

170

As Christians, we are the beloved of God. We can stake our claim on that promised land. We can choose to trust it and allow it to change us, or we can mistrust it. Not trusting it doesn't make it any less true. It simply makes it untrue for us. It keeps us locked out of the freedom of experiencing God's embrace. It's like being invited to a party and mistrusting the invitation. The party is going on with or without us. Should we choose not to attend, we are the ones who lose.

Understanding who we are in Christ intellectually will not change us unless we *trust* that identity in the core of our being. We are completely and totally loved and embraced in the arms of God. Allowing that relationship to transform us is the key. Doctors Les and Leslie Parrott have warned us, "If you try to find intimacy with another person before achieving a sense of identity on your own, all your relationships become an attempt to complete yourself."

No woman thinks she is doing this. We usually can't see that we've done it until our relationship disappoints us in some way. We may feel betrayed, or lonely, or dissatisfied, and so be confronted by how much we depended on the relationship to make us whole.

We could feel threatened. Fear of loss causes a fierce reaction. If you are dating someone and that person begins to pull away, you might be faced with strong feelings of rejection that cause you to question your worth. How much of your identity did you build on that relationship? With the possibility of losing that person, you realize that you trusted him for more than companionship or intimacy. You trusted him to complete you.

> "We always deceive ourselves about the people we love—first to their advantage, then to their disadvantage."
> —Albert Camus

We do find a *sense* of completion in relationship. We are drawn to those who possess qualities that we don't have. We long to find someone who fits us and makes us feel "whole." But on another level, "wholeness" in relationship is impossible with two very flawed human beings. It's like two ticks with no dog, each trying to get from the other what they need to fill them up. It can be incredibly satisfying, but not for long. Unfortunately, the satisfying part usually lasts through the courtship. We cannot enter into relationship to take away loneliness; we will discover quickly that it doesn't work. The only thing worse than being single and lonely is being married and lonely.

We are not bad people for trying to find someone else to complete us. We will be disappointed people, and frustrated people, and angry people, but we are not bad people. It's simply that no one else can fit in the place that God designed for Himself.

Giving ourselves to God affords us the opportunity to enter relationship with a spiritual foundation to build on. Another person is not a strong enough base.

Directed Journaling

- Does trusting come easily for you? Write why you think you struggle with trust, or why you think you don't.
- Pick two of the chapters that we have walked back through and write in detail what you can do to put more trust in those areas of your relationship.

Enrich Your Relationships by Interviewing Others' Anger

Hopefully you are on your way to becoming Barbara Walters to your soul. When you find fear or frustration or hurt

172

feelings, you are taking note and trying to get to the bottom of it. You are asking yourself good questions and seeking to answer them honestly. You will change your relationships if you truly trust this principle in your own life.

But there is more: take this cup of fresh-brewed life that you have sipped from and offer it to your mate. If you have learned how to interview your anger, or you are committed to trying, then use the process with those that you love. If your husband or boyfriend is hiding anger or something is smoldering underneath the surface, help him get to the bottom of it. Ask probing questions that can help him uncover his anger.

Very important: you can't help him if you are angry. This principle will not work if you are in a heated argument or you are the one he's in conflict with. It takes softness and tenderness to ask deep questions. Try to move to the place of uncovering the tender hurt in his soul. "Where does it hurt?" is always a good question, not only for yourself, but for others. "What do you need from me right now?" can move you from an impasse to an honest place of knowing how to help.

The interview process is a critical tool for good communication. The quicker we can get to the heart of the issue, the more quickly and less painfully it can be resolved. It's the "hard hurt" that causes the wounds. You have to get beneath it as quickly as possible. When Paul picks up a sword and starts swinging, and I pick up mine, a fight will ensue. But if I stand unarmed, afraid, but trusting that we can get to the soft hurt, I usually emerge without too many cuts. I can ask a well-placed interview question and change the course of our evening. When I take the battle route, we both can be bloody for days.

Enriching Your Relationship by Encountering Your Journal

Journaling is like free counseling for your relationship. As journaling helps us ferret out the negative, destructive voices

In the last three centuries, 90 percent of all people living in the Western world have switched from tea to coffee.

that go on in our souls, it can only help our relationships. When we bring a more awake, authentic, living self to any relationship, satisfaction is increased tenfold. When we bring our hearts to God on paper and spill out our souls before Him, it will impact our relationships to the core. If we are learning from our lives by listening and responding and letting God direct us, the special person in our lives will reap incredible benefits.

For example, when I have an argument with Paul, and I am angry, my journal is the place where I conduct the interview. As I am fuming, I need a place to process. I begin to write over and over

> "Love does not consist in gazing at each other, but in looking together in the same direction."
> —Antoine de Saint-Exupéry

how wrong he was, how mad he made me, how I don't want to forgive him, and on the twelfth time, I see plain as day how wrong *I* was. Then I write what really happened. I peel back another layer, and write about what I did, and perhaps why I did it. Sometimes I have to ask God to show me why I said what I said or did such a mean thing. If I don't wrestle it out in my journal, I can easily miss seeing what I have done or the real reason I have done it. The latter is what I am after. Paul can try to point out what I have done, but that doesn't always work. For me to see it and understand why I did it is pretty critical to it not happening again (at least not in the next twenty-four hours).

Paul wants me to write in my journal. And I want him to write in his. Sometimes when we have a big enough argument to warrant a "time-out," we'll both grab our journals and spend the time writing. By the time we come back together, each of us is ready to apologize. God has convicted each of us, and our journaling moves us toward taking the responsibility for the relationship.

God has access to my heart through my journal. He meets me in the midst of my writing, and He teaches me about relationship. It is in my journal that I wrestle with issues of forgiveness. It is in my writing time that I pray for Paul. God brings things to my mind that I can pray for him about. I write out my prayers for him, sometimes like love letters. Journaling is a structured way to pray for your loved ones, and we know that when we begin to pray, God does amazing things.

Fresh-Brewed Adventures

- Go to a nice restaurant or just stay in, but find a quiet place to spend an evening with your spouse or boyfriend talking about the good things in your relationship. Discuss the cups of fresh-brewed life. Ask which one he would like to see enriching more of your relationship. Just listen; you might be surprised by what he says.
- Spend time journaling about your relationship. What principle will ever change your life until you commit to do it? What does your relationship need more of? How can you begin to make the necessary changes? Begin with prayer for God's help.
- Celebrate your relationship with a party. Plan something fun. Use the suggestions for celebration from the friendship chapter and go all out. Not expensive, not a lot of people necessarily—just make sure you have the things that "count."

Enriching Your Relationship by Changing Your World Together

Henri Nouwen said: "Marriage is foremost a vocation. Two people are called together to fulfill the mission that God has given them. That is to say, a man and a woman come together for life, not just because they experience deep love for each other, but because they believe that God loves each of them with an infinite love and has called them to each other to be living witnesses of that love."

We show God's love to each other in relationship. When we forgive each other, that is a sign of God's forgiveness of us. We are never more like God than when we forgive others. Relationships afford us our greatest opportunity to model the gospel. We are called to be light-bearers in a dark world that only recognizes one language: love. The Scripture tells us that the world will only recognize us as followers of Christ by the love that we have for one another.

There is nothing more powerful than seeing a couple who love each other working side by side to communicate that love to the world. This communication happens far more by what they do than by what they say. To stand together with another individual in love—with one mission, purpose, and passion—speaks volumes.

To enrich your relationship, begin to pray about your mission as a couple. As you have discovered your "one thing" that drives you in serving God, encourage your spouse to discover his "one thing" as well. Many times there is a mission that comes from combining both of your passions. This will change your relationship and the world around you! Whether it is teaching a Bible study together, or hammering with Habitat for Humanity to build houses, or just going on an overseas trip together to work—something electric happens when you combine forces. All of a sudden one plus one doesn't equal two; it equals twelve.

Enriching Your Relationship by Listening to Your Longings

I had my wisdom teeth out about five years ago. They were causing me to have headaches and jaw pain. When they extract a tooth, especially an impacted (surrounded by bone) tooth, it leaves a gaping hole. (I know, I'm oversharing.) They removed my teeth and sent me home with four rather large holes in my head. I had pain medicine and a list of instructions from the doctor for Paul. I don't remember much about that day, as I spent all of it in bed. But around 8:00 P.M. I awoke to the burglar alarm going off. Paul was sleeping soundly next to me. First, I wondered why he was in bed so early, and second, I wondered how come I was the one hearing the alarm through pain medication. So, I woke him up. My cheeks were very swollen, and I was not talking very clearly. I told him, "The burglar alarm . . . the burglar alarm." He said to me, "Turn it off." And he rolled over and went back to sleep. I was keenly aware that although we'd had an alarm system for five years, we'd never talked about what to do if it went off! I woke him up again. "We can't turn it off; there might be a burglar." I wanted him to go and check. He said, "I'm not going to check; there might be a burglar!" Finally, the police arrived and checked the house. The motion detector had been set off by a "get-well" balloon. No burglars.

That would have been a relief were it not for the pain. Searing, throbbing, aching pain. In the excitement of the wake-up call, I had jumped out of bed and rushed to activity, unaware of anything but the alarm. But when I lay back down to go to sleep, my head was on fire. I took more medicine, but it didn't help. I had not slept much by the next morning when I crawled the next morning back to the doctor.

I'd developed dry socket. The holes where my teeth had been were dry and no moisture could get to them. And the holes started howling. The pain was very intense. It's the kind of pain that wraps around your ears, pushes out your eyes, keeps you from walking straight, and makes you say very mean things to your husband. To alleviate the pain, the oral surgeon mercifully inserted a coated gauze. As soon as the holes were filled, they stopped screaming. The pain was gone. It would have been a miracle cure, except for the cloves. The coating on the gauze was a clove mixture so strong it will make you swear off the spice the rest of your life (I still can't eat clove-studded ham). No more pain, but terrible taste. But the holes can't heal with the gauze in. Eventually the stuffing must come out, and I would be left to deal with the holes.

I went through three different cycles of dry socket, stuff the holes, choke on the cloves, remove the gauze, screaming pain . . . stuff the holes, choke . . . By the third time, I had learned a lesson about relationships.

I grew up watching *The Love Boat* and *Fantasy Island*. So surely you can understand that even though I was a Christian, I thought that my *husband* would make me happy. Don't misunderstand, he does make me happy—but not all the time. I thought he would be the fulfillment of my deepest longings. And he does fulfill many of my dreams—but not all the time. I thought he would complete me—and all the empty places in my life would be filled—all the time. I wanted someone to be my happiness, the fulfiller of my longings *all the time*.

And then one day the alarm went off. I was in pain. I realized that he couldn't meet all of my needs, or complete me. I was left with just me. I found empty places with nothing to fill them. Longings. They began to throb and scream and howl and wrap around my ears and push out my eyes,

> "There is no fear in love. But perfect love drives out fear."
> —1 John 4:18

keeping me from walking straight and making me say mean things to my husband.

As I listened, I heard a longing for a father. That was one of the holes in my life. When it ached, I asked Paul to fill it, but he could not. I heard a longing in my soul to be known. When it ached, I was mad at Paul because he hadn't filled it. By really listening to my longings, I realized that I was longing for God. Another human being had just as many holes as I did. And some of the holes overlapped. We were empty in the same places.

Paul and I were going through a tough time this spring. I was acutely aware, again, that I had brought some of my longings to him to fill. People are not the fulfillers of longings. God is. If we fail to listen to our longings, we continually place others in the position of being painkilling gauze that will fill holes but not move us any closer to healing. On one particular Sunday, in the midst of profound disappointment in myself and in my relationship with Paul, God asked me a very pointed question: "Do you stay married because you love Paul, or do you stay married because you love Me?" I wept as I answered, "Because I love you, God."

"Then trust Me to meet your longings as I choose."

Recipe

Cappuccino Cheesecake

Chocolate Crumb Crust

1 tablespoon butter
1 package (9 ounces) dark chocolate wafer cookies, finely ground
Pinch of cinnamon
1/3 cup melted butter

Coat bottom and sides of a 9-inch springform pan with 1 tablespoon butter. In a food processor using the steel blade, combine cookie crumbs, cinnamon, and melted butter. Press crumb mixture evenly on sides and bottom of prepared pan. Bake at 325° for 5 minutes. Cool.

Filling

1 1/4 pounds cream cheese, cut into 1-inch cubes

1 1/4 cups sugar

4 eggs, beaten

3/4 cup whipping cream

3/4 cup sour cream

1 ounce semisweet chocolate, finely chopped

1/4 cup espresso

3 tablespoons Kahlua

1 teaspoon vanilla

Using the steel blade of a food processor, combine cream cheese, sugar, and eggs until smooth. Scrape sides down and add whipping cream and sour cream. Process to combine. Melt chocolate with espresso in the microwave and cool. Add chocolate mixture, liqueur, and vanilla to cream cheese mixture. Pour into prepared crust. Bake at 325° for 1 hour and 15 minutes, or until sides of the cake are set 2 inches in from the edges and center of cake is still pudding-like. Remove cake from oven and let cool on a wire rack until room temperature. Refrigerate cake overnight. Serves 8–12.

Enrich Your Relationship by Celebrating Friendship

Paul and I are business partners. We've worked together for eleven years. But we did not marry to be business partners. We perform live theater sketches all over the country. But we did not marry to act together. We married to be lifelong friends and to have fun together. We married for companionship. There have been times in our marriage when we were better business partners than companions. Just this last year, we realized, again, that we were not cultivating the friendship in our marriage. We both know that if we don't consciously take time to celebrate the friendship that we have, it will be gone. But knowing must translate to doing.

Once in relationship, men tend to slack off in the pursuit of friendship. I don't know if this is a retro characteristic that goes back to their caveman days or what. But for some reason they don't seem to pursue us as much after we say "I do." Perhaps there is no more thrill in the chase, no more adventure in the hunt when they know they have us. For whatever reason, and whether they take responsibility for it or not, if they slough off the friendship, we have to pick up the ball. Keeping a friendship alive is crucial. Friends talk and laugh, and give cards and flowers and surprises. We can do that.

The number one reason that women have affairs is for friendship. If you want to affair-proof your marriage, make sure you are having fun together. If the friendship dies in your marriage or relationship, it's going to be tough sledding. Girlfriends offer friendship to us that our man cannot, but to exclude friendship with your mate because you are finding it with your girlfriends can hurt your relationship. The friendship with our mate needs to be celebrated too. That may mean it's up to us. Knowing that you need a healthy friendship must be translated into creating one.

Our lives as women are full of demands: raising kids, working, providing shuttle service, coordinating schedules, grocery shopping. These tasks can cause us to function in relationship more like business partners than passionate friends. And if a business partner isn't pulling his weight or doing his share, you replace him. With the loss of friendship, for many women and men, it becomes that simple. Find someone else. That is never a real solution, but it can seem like one to the woman who has

> "If you cannot inspire a woman with love of you, fill her above the brim with love of herself; all that runs over will be yours."
> —Charles Caleb Colton

lost her friend. Rather than finding yourself dealing with that dilemma, celebrate your friendship with your mate.

Enrich Your Relationship by Embracing Your Beauty

Mary, my right-hand assistant in our office, picked up a trunk for us from the airport. She had picked it up on Sunday in Jennifer's car but forgot to load it into her own car. When Mary came in to work on Monday, she realized that she had forgotten it. On Tuesday, she was embarrassed that she still had not gotten it out of Jennifer's car. She wrote herself a note to transfer the trunk so she would have it for us Wednesday morning. When I got to the office, I asked her about the trunk. She started laughing and said that Jennifer had loaded the trunk into her car on Sunday night! She'd had the trunk for two days and didn't even know it.

To trust that we are beautiful means we may not see it, but we trust it's there. Not trusting *in* it. Trusting that we have it. Beauty is an issue of faith. We have to choose sides. If we believe that we have beauty, and embrace it, then we allow what is inside us to come out. If we doubt that we possess it, we will try to obtain it apart from ourselves, and the pressure is on to find it and bring it inside us.

I can put tremendous pressure on Paul when I don't embrace my beauty and trust it. I can render him terrified with one question: "How does my hair look?" He would rather solve any crisis in the Middle East than have to answer that question. He knows it's a setup. My attitude toward the evening could be riding on his answer. And if he stops to think about it, he's taken too long, and he's in trouble.

Once, when I asked Paul how my hair looked, he said, "What do you want me to say?" I said, "Not that!" We want men to "know." We want them to say the things that will help us out of a self-esteem jam.

Men are in a tough spot because they can't win one way or the other. We are looking to them to ease our fears, or reassure us, or confirm our worst fears. "Do these pants make my butt look big?" How in the world can a man answer that question? Maybe you have a big butt already, and you know it, so why are you asking him? Sometimes I think we teach our husbands to lie to us. And then we get mad at them when they don't do it very well. We'd really like to blame them, when it's our fault for setting them up.

Karen Lee-Thorp and Cynthia Hicks wrote, "The man who nags his wife about her appearance or leaves her for a younger woman has yielded to idolatry. On the other hand, a man who lovingly confronts his wife for showing no concern about her appearance, or for endangering her health through overeating, is doing his job. The line between nagging and confronting may be blurry; it's up to each man and woman to examine their motives."

Can we let our husbands lovingly confront us when it comes to beauty? Or do we constantly question their motives and their hearts? We can only let them in to enjoy our beauty when we have embraced it ourselves. We can trust them if we are not trusting *in* them to determine our worth. We can trust our husband or our boyfriend if we have learned that our beauty comes from God. Then the husband or boyfriend is free to reap the benefits of our trusting.

Enrich Your Relationship by Savoring Your Sexuality

Paul and I were sitting in Ken's office rehashing a fight we'd had the night before. A leftover fight is a cold, tasteless thing. We were picking at it and pushing it around on the plate. It was a fight about sex. Paul explained to Ken why I was wrong and what I had done. I countered to defend myself and to clearly communicate Paul's missteps in our argument. Before

Paul could get out a snappy comeback, Ken stopped us. "What assumptions are you making right now about each other?" he asked.

We looked back at him blankly.

"Nicole, do you think Paul loves you?"

"Yes," I admitted honestly, "but what he did . . ."

Ken cut me off. "Wait. Paul, do you think Nicole was trying to hurt you on purpose?"

"It felt that way . . . but no."

"Do you think she loves you and that her heart toward you is good?"

"Yes," Paul answered.

"Neither of you acted as if you were loved. You acted out of the fear that the other didn't care for you."

He was right. I didn't trust Paul's heart. Each of us was trying to uncover some sinister plot that the other had to wreck our evening. But there were no plots. Just misunder-

> "Marriage is our last, best chance to grow up."
>
> —Joseph Barth

standings from bad communication. We had assumed the worst in the other, and it caused us to react in a way that hurt our relationship. We missed out on a great evening because we had mistrusted. I know Paul loves me, but if I assume that he doesn't, I begin to see it everywhere. It is difficult enough to really savor your sexuality when you have a great relationship, but it's downright impossible if you aren't trusting each other. How can you give yourself to someone who might not have your best interest at heart? We must trust that our mate's heart toward us is good, in order to savor our sexuality.

This is easier said than done. Especially if you have been in relationships in which people's hearts toward you were not good. You can very easily project false assumptions and sinister motives on your mate and hurt your relationship deeply.

184

You can withdraw to protect yourself, only to discover you are hiding from the one who loves you. Sex isn't about hiding, it's about revealing, and in order to reveal we must give our trust.

C. S. Lewis said: "Of all powers, love is the most powerful and the most powerless. It is the most powerful because it alone can conquer that final and most impregnable stronghold which is the human heart. It is the most powerless because it can do nothing except by consent."

Everyone has a story of how trust was broken and why he or she can't trust. Not trusting comes naturally. Actually trusting came first, and then sadly we learned to distrust. Once we distrust, it is hard to go back to trusting again. But the path of enriching our relationships is a way of trust. It is the only road that leads from knowing to doing.

But what about people who aren't trustworthy? Are you supposed to trust even when you might get hurt? What if someone has let you down? How can you trust that person, and should you? When we distrust we hurt ourselves. If you trust someone and he lets you down, were you wrong for trusting? Or was that person wrong for letting you down? Just because you trusted him doesn't make you foolish. If anything, we can be proud of the fact that we trusted.

> "The Eskimo has fifty-two names for snow because it is important to them: there ought to be as many for love."
>
> —Margaret Atwood,
> Canadian writer

It's much like that with love. When we love someone who doesn't love us, are we fools? Or are we better people for having loved, even if that love wasn't returned? When we learn to trust others, we are changed in the process. We trust because of what it does for us, not because of what it does for the other person.

When we have a problem with trusting, we must ask ourselves this question: *If I trust this person, and he lets me down, what is the worst thing that could happen?* The answer usually reveals the fear that keeps us from trusting. Some of us would rather mistrust another individual and be right than gain the benefit of trusting and be wrong about the person. I choose to believe the best and be sad when I am mistaken rather than believe the worst and seek to find confirmation. Not trusting doesn't make you the winner. To be disfigured by mistrust makes you the loser every time.

185

This is not to say we will not be scarred in the process of learning to trust. Trusting is bloody. When Jacob wrestled with the angel, he was learning to trust, and it left him limping. Oftentimes in our battle to trust we have to wrestle with the deepest, darkest, worst fears. We must wrestle them to the ground, and then we trust. For example, if you are trying to trust God for financial provision, ask yourself, *What is the worst thing that could happen?* Could you still trust God if that happened? If you can wrestle that fear to the ground and know that God is still there in the quietness of the dark, then you are on your way to trusting on a whole new level.

When we trust others, we reveal that we trust God and that we trust ourselves. We have not placed our hope in others' trustworthiness. We have placed our hope in a Savior who is completely able to come through for us. We do not demand demonstrations of others' ability to be trusted, because our ultimate trust is not in other people. That is not to say that we don't want others to do what they say they will or strive to honor their word, but it is to say we know that, ultimately, there will be times when others will let us down. They will disappoint us and frustrate us, but we can choose to believe that their hearts toward us are good. We can bring trust to our relationships to enrich them with action and endow them with meaning.

In the ancient Arab world, coffee became such a staple in family life that one of the causes allowed by law for marital separation was a husband's refusal to produce coffee for his wife.

186

We trust because we can't live a fresh-brewed life without it. None of the cups of the chapters that precede this one will really wake us up without trusting. We can know them backward and forward, upside down and right side up, but until we put weight on them and trust, our souls will still be sleepy. The wake-up call is a call to surrender, listen, interview, pursue, encounter, embrace, celebrate, savor, surrender, and trust.

Conclusion
SHARING A CUP

My mother's mother, Audrey, introduced me to coffee. She would make me coffee-milk in the mornings before anyone else got up. I must have been four or five, and, holding my current favorite stuffed companion and still sucking my thumb, I would pad sleepy-eyed into the kitchen where the kettle was boiling. The only light in the room was the one on the stove, and my grandmother would be sitting on a stool next to the counter, sipping coffee. She would get up and begin to fix my coffee-milk. Sweet and warm beyond compare. Sharing a cup became our secret ritual. I thought it was my reward for waking up early. She would pull me up a chair, and we would talk for a bit. I felt so grown up.

Years later would find me in junior high sitting around a huge table in Alabama with my dad's family, observing the coffee ritual, but not participating yet. I wasn't old enough. My father's brothers and sisters needed nothing more than a coffeepot for celebration. Okay, maybe one of Grandma's caramel cakes helped a bit. They would sit for hours with coffee and one another. I would take it all in, learning what "coffee" meant to them: love, sharing, and connection.

I didn't discover coffee again until college. Too many papers and not enough evening sent me searching for caffeine. I returned to my coffee-milk days with MaMa Audrey. I found warmth and security, holding this dark brew in my hands. I returned to my father's family's table in Alabama as a coffee drinker and an adult. It was, and still is, the best way to join in a good conversation with them.

I haven't finished fresh-brewed life. Even though our time together is drawing to a close as I write these last pages, I know I will never be "finished" with this book. Writing about living freshly has served as a more intense wake-up call. I will continue going back over these chapters and drinking from these cups. I encourage you to do the same. I want to stay alive and awake, and that comes from surrendering to God, encountering my journal, listening to my longings, embracing my beauty, interviewing my anger, savoring my sexuality, celebrating my friendships, changing my world, and enriching my relationships as much as I can, as often as I can.

Seeking to stay awake is not a frantic, caffeine-induced alertness, but a consistent, gentle stirring. Keep going back to your whole-bean essence, submitting to being finely ground and allowing God's passion to make the freshest brewed life you can know.

As you get the hang of making a cup, allow God to make a pot. Share a cup of fresh-brewed life. Put enough grounds in the filter to make more than you need. There is a world that desperately needs your fresh-brewed life. Remember, God wastes nothing. Not your sorrows, nor your joys. Throw it all in the filter and let Him brew it. Then share a cup with the world.

BIBLIOGRAPHY

Ban Breathnach, Sarah. *Simple Abundance.* New York: Warner Books, 1995.

Buford, Bob. *Half Time.* Grand Rapids, MI: Zondervan, 1994.

Dewberry, Elizabeth. "Praying for a Home: Some Thoughts on Writing and God." *Image* Number 15: 64, 66.

Dillard, Annie. *Teaching a Stone to Talk.* New York: Harper Perennial, 1982.

Douglas, Susan J. *Where the Girls Are: Growing Up Female with the Mass Media.* New York: Random House, 1995.

Griffin, Emilie. *Clinging: The Experience of Prayer.* New York: McCracken Press, 1994.

Groom, Nancy. *Heart to Heart About Men.* Colorado Springs, CO: NavPress, 1995.

Katona, Christie and Tom Katona. *The Coffee Book.* San Leandro, CA: Bristol Publishing, 1992.

Kidd, Sue Monk. *When the Heart Waits*. San Francisco: Harper-Row, 1990.

Lee-Thorp, Karen and Cynthia Hicks. *Why Beauty Matters*. Colorado Springs, CO: NavPress, 1997.

L'Engle, Madeline. *Walking on Water*. Wheaton, IL: Harold Shaw Publishers, 1972.

Lerner, Harriet Goldhor. *The Dance of Anger*. New York: Harper and Row, 1985.

Nouwen, Henri. *Life of the Beloved: Spiritual Living in a Secular World*. New York: Crossroad, 1992.

———. *Here and Now: Living in the Spirit*. New York: Crossroad, 1994.

O'Connor, Elizabeth. *Letters to Scattered Pilgrims*. New York: Harper and Row, 1979.

Parrott, Les and Leslie Parrott. *Relationships*. Grand Rapids, MI: Zondervan, 1998.

SARK. *Succulent Wild Woman*. New York: Simon and Schuster, 1997.

Wells, Ann. "A Story to Live By," *Los Angeles Times*, 1997.

ABOUT THE AUTHOR

Nicole Johnson is an actor, author, and sought-after speaker. Traveling nationally with the Women of Faith conferences, Nicole performs original dramatic sketches on the issues facing women today.

Nicole can be contacted through:

Women of Faith
820 Spring Creek Parkway, Suite 400
Plano, TX 75023

Fresh-Brewed Life is also available on video as a small-group study, complete with a video guide and an EZ Lesson Plan. Call Thomas Nelson at 1-800-251-4000 and ask for Nelson Word Direct, or e-mail us at NelsonWordDirect@ThomasNelson.com. For information, please include your area code so that your questions are directed to the appropriate representatives.